D1595334

DIVINE WILL and
HUMAN EXPERIENCE:

Explorations of the Halakhic System and Its Values

by Rabbi Aryeh Klapper, Dean

published by
CENTER FOR MODERN TORAH LEADERSHIP

© 2022 Aryeh Klapper

ISBN 978-1-66785-143-3

PART I
METAHALAKHIC PRINCIPLES

PART III
HALAKHIC METHODS

PART IV
LONG COVID AND YOM KIPPUR

PART V
HALAKHIC ILLUSTRATIONS

6

PART VI
BIBLICAL PORTRAITS

PART
I

METAHALAKHIC PRINCIPLES

Chapter 1

WHAT THE CREATION AND EXODUS NARRATIVES TEACH ABOUT HALAKHAH

Freedom isn't a zero-sum game – there can be more or less freedom in the world. It's also not an altruistic game – giving up my freedom may diminish rather than increase yours. Different kinds of freedom may limit each other - consider Isaiah Berlin's essential distinction between "freedom from" and "freedom to". Freedom is complicated.

Let's start with a G-d's-eye perspective. When G-d was all that existed, His "freedom from" was absolute. The angels argued against creating humanity because the existence of beings with any degree of freedom would diminish His.

But G-d chose to create humanity anyway. Why? Because the absence of other free-willed beings limited his "freedom to." He could not express generosity or be loved.

Rav Yosef Dov Soloveitchik argued that the Biblical story of Creation should be read as normative. Human beings are charged with being as much like G-d as we can be. To begin with: just as He created, so too we must create.

Having read Nietzsche, the Rav also recognized the danger of this idea. What if human beings realize that to be truly like G-d we must be absolutely autonomous, create our own norms? Why would we be wrong?

One answer is that human beings cannot truly be like G-d. Imitatio dei is a permanent aspiration but cannot actually be achieved.

A second answer is that human beings exist in the world that G-d created, and in which G-d exists. So we can never have the freedom that G-d had before Creation. We can never be the only free-willed being in existence. This fantasy of unbounded freedom is what led Kayin to murder Hevel, only to rediscover G-d.

The issue between these two answers is the proper relationship between narrative and nomos. The first answer contends that the 613 commandments must be understood in light of their normative preamble, the story of Creation. In other words, halakhah's purpose is to maximize freedom in a world where perfect freedom is impossible. The second answer contends that the normative story of Creation must be interpreted in light of the subsequent 613 commandments. It is possible for halakhah, properly interpreted, to limit or diminish freedom.

I prefer a third answer. The normative message of Creation is complex. G-d's creation **limited** His own freedom in one sense while expanding it in another.

The existence of other free-willed beings meant that G-d entered the sphere of ethics; in a sense we can say that He acquired **duties** toward us. Duties toward others restrict the freedom of one's own will. This may be the underlying message of all the Rabbinic stories that portray G-d observing the mitzvot.

On the other hand, by enabling Hashem to act ethically, to express *middot* such as *chesed,* Creation also expanded Divine "freedom to."

On this reading, the existence of mitzvot is not in tension with the norm of creation. Rather, mitzvot should be understood as opportunities to expand our "freedom to."

The challenge is that acknowledging the existence of a normative **obligation** always carries with it the *yetzer hora* to impose that obligation on others against their will, to violate their "freedom from" in the name of their "freedom to". But mitzvot done in submission to another human will rarely develop new virtues in the coerced.

It turns out that there are two religious paths to becoming a slave-owner.

The first is the Nietzschean/Fascist temptation, the belief that your freedom to obey G-d is limited to the extent that others have any capacity to limit your actions, and expanded by the capacity to have others do your will. An alternative manifestation is the belief that it is worth submerging your individual identity into a collective that is free from external constraints. The truth is that your "freedom to" is even more limited by your inability to relate to other beings as free.

Moreover, the effort to keep others subjugated will end up controlling your life, whether as an individual or as a society.

The second route to slaveownership is the anti-Nietszchean/Communist/Puritan temptation, the belief that freedom is not intrinsically valuable at all, and certainly not as valuable as obedience to G-d. So it is better for others' wills to be subordinated to mine, and thereby certainly to G-d's, than for them to be left free, which risks their disobeying G-d.

These two paths are ideologically opposed, but perfectly complementary in practice. They parallel the first two explanations above of the relationship between Creation and Mitzvot.

The narrative of *yetziyat mitzrayim* seems the antidote to these ideological poisons. Here the point is as clear as can be – G-d hates slavery, and He intervenes to end it. As Rashi famously points out, the Exodus is really a second Creation. Before Creation, there was no time, and time restarts at the Exodus, with a normative component:

"This month/newness/chodesh must be for you the head of months; it shall be the first for you, of the months of the year."

Rashi therefore asks: Why is the narrative of the first Creation necessary? I suggest: because otherwise we might not realize that creativity is intrinsically valuable.

But the narrative of Exodus can also be normatively misunderstood. We can argue that the story is not about generic freedom from *avdut*, but only about Jewish freedom from Gentile *avdut*. On this misreading, our goal is to become *avdei Hashem* in the sense of slaves rather than free-willed servants, and we are entitled to enslave others to increase our and their obedience to G-d. (Both *yitzrei hora* at once!) After all, the regulations of *avdut* follow almost immediately after the Ten Commandments, with their preamble

"I am Hashem your G-d
Who took out of Mitzrayim, from the house of avadim."

Is this juxtaposition intended to teach us to read the preamble narrowly?

No! Exactly the opposite! The juxtaposition emphasizes that the entire Torah framework of law, society, halakhah – all of which constrain some sorts of freedom – must nonetheless be understood as having the purpose of maximizing freedom, and must be interpreted accordingly. Sometimes the world leaves human beings very few choices, if any, to keep themselves and their families alive. With full awareness of the dangers (we call it *avdut!*), halakhah sets up a mechanism to ameliorate such situations and enable at least some degree of freedom in the present, and to guarantee that the prospect of freedom is always present.

This reading is demonstrated by Yirmiyahu 34:13-14, which states that the law that an *eved ivri* must be freed embodies the covenant Hashem made with the Jews on the day He took them out of Egypt. Note that the law itself allows an *eved* contract to last six years, but the language of 34:9-10 implies that Yirmiyah demanded immediate manumission.

In the Yerushalmi (Rosh HaShannah 3:5), Rav Shmuel son of Rav Yitzchak argues, against Rashi, that the norm must precede creation. Shemot 6:13 states:

וַיְדַבֵּר יְקוָק אֶל־מֹשֶׁה וְאֶל־אַהֲרֹן
וַיְצַוֵּם אֶל־בְּנֵי יִשְׂרָאֵל
וְאֶל־פַּרְעֹה מֶלֶךְ מִצְרָיִם
לְהוֹצִיא אֶת־בְּנֵי־יִשְׂרָאֵל מֵאֶרֶץ מִצְרָיִם.

Hashem spoke to Mosheh and Aharon
He commanded them regarding Benei Yisroel
and regarding Pharaoh King of Mitzrayim
to bring Benei Yisroel *out of Mitzrayim.*

What was the content of this command? The laws of freeing slaves, as referenced by Yirmiyahu.

Some contemporary rabbinic commentators note that Yirmiyahu refers to the covenant being established on the day of the Exodus, whereas this verse apparently takes place long before then. Their suggestion is that even though this mitzvah became binding law only at the Exodus, the command was given at the very beginning of redemption. The Jews needed to know the meaning of G-d's intervention before it happened, and before they received the Torah. That meaning can be expressed as follows:

אין בן חורין אלא מי שעוסק בתורה

ואין בן תורה אלא מי שעוסק בחרות

Only those who engage in Torah can be free;

Only those who engage in maximizing freedom can be bnei Torah.

Chapter 2

CHAZAKOT AND CHANGING REALITIES

Practical Halakhah exists in constant dialogue with the world around it. Competent poskim know and respond to the social, political, and economic realities of their communities. In turn, halakhah shapes those realities in important ways. Consider for example the effect of capitalism on the halakhot of *ribbit* (usury), and the effect of halakhah on the price of ungrafted citrons.

Igrot Mosheh EH 1:49 was written while Rav Mosheh Feinstein was living in Luban, Belarus. Most of Rav Feinstein's teshuvot from that period were lost in transit to America (see the biography printed at the start of Igrot Mosheh vol. 8). The ones that survive often establish themes that recur in his halakhic decisions. In general, while Rav Mosheh's specific halakhic positions sometimes shifted over time, his underlying commitments were rock-solid. One of those commitments was to freeing agunot, and more, to an expansive notion of what constitutes a situation of iggun.

Let's see how Rav Mosheh implemented that commitment in full awareness of the changing realities around him.

Belarus joined the USSR in 1922, and Stalin came to power in 1924. The new combination of totalitarianism and ideological opposition to religion changed the reality of agunah cases in three ways. First, many women had a real option of leaving the religious community if the rabbis refused them permission to remarry. Second, even women who stayed within the community might see halakhah on this issue as an obstacle course rather than as a substantive moral guide. Third, husbands might be "disappeared" forever without notice and without record. Each of these factors potentially altered the halakhic calculus of credibility regarding a woman's claim that her husband had died

Two valid direct witnesses are ordinarily necessary to undo a presumption of marriage However, Mishnah Yebamot 15:1 states that if a married couple goes abroad, and the woman returns alone claiming to be widowed, she is believed, even if her claim is based on hearsay. The Talmud explains that the standards of evidence are relaxed because "the rabbis were lenient in order to free agunot". The rabbis also added severe penalties for fraud or error: if the first husband turns up alive after the woman remarries with permission from a beit din, she is forbidden to both men, her children from the second marriage are considered mamzerim, and further children from the first husband will be considered mamzerim. Those penalties reinforce an underlying *chazokoh* , or legal presumption, that women investigate comprehensively before they remarry.

Rav Mosheh's interlocutor questions whether this *chazokoh* is still applicable. He provides an example where halakhic presumptions about credibility have changed over time. In the Talmud, a woman is believed if she claims to be divorced while in her presumptive husband's presence. The ground for believing her is a *chazokoh* attributed to Rav Hamnuna that "A woman is not brazen in the presence of her husband". But Rav Mosheh Isserles (RAMO) in his glosses to Shulchan Arukh Even HaEzer 17:2 rules that because of societal changes, this *chazokoh* no longer generates the credibility necessary to allow remarriage. Perhaps the same is true for the *chazokoh* that woman investigate comprehensively before they remarry?

Rav Mosheh responds with an emphatic no. The changes that led RAMO to sideline Rav Hamnuna's *chazokoh* regarding divorce have no necessary implications for the *chazokoh* regarding death.

Rav Mosheh's response ignores - I suggest deliberately - the question of whether changes specific to his own time and place have weakened the latter chazokoh. Everything he says could have been written identically in the late 16th century.

Two halakhic issues remain, however.

The first is that the Mishnah says that the widow is believed only if "there is peace in the world and peace among them". If there is war, then perhaps the husband is alive and prevented from returning or communicating. If there was marital strife, then perhaps the husband is maliciously staying out of contact precisely to make his wife an agunah. Rav Mosheh notes that in our case, even by the woman's account, the husband had been completely out of touch for twenty years before his death. That seems to show clearly that he was in fact willing and maybe eager to leave her an agunah. So why is she given halakhic credibility?

Rav Mosheh offers three responses.

The first is entirely technical. Talmud Yebamot 116a limits "lack of peace between them" to the extreme case in which the wife has previously made a false claim of divorce. RAMO EH 17:48 cites a position that adds the case of a husband who apostasized. Rav Mosheh argues that while RAMO adds another case where the wife is not believed, he does not intend to broaden the category of "lack of peace between them" beyond the one case in the Talmud. He contends that this is the better reading of RAMO's source in Shiltei Gibborim. (I am not sure why.)

His second response is that in this case, there are witnesses that the woman behaved as a widow the moment she reported the husband's death. He contends that this enhances her credibility. (I am not sure why.)

His third response is that even RAMO's extension is controversial.

Rav Mosheh does not specifically address whether the gulag might play the same role as "lack of peace in the world".

Overall, Rav Mosheh's responses seem weak if his goal is to convince us that the woman is obviously being truthful. However, they make a great deal of sense in light of MAHARIK #72.

MAHARIK notes that Mishnah Yebamot 15:2 frames the decision to relax the standards of evidence as resulting from a specific case in which a beit din investigated a woman's claim to be widowed and it proved true. Tosafot Yebamot 116b comment: "because they saw that there would be many agunot if they did not believe her". Maharik explains that the specific case taught the Rabbis that even women who told the truth would often be unable to find sufficient formal evidence. The Rabbis knew that some women would falsely claim to be widows; it would be ridiculous to conclude from one case that all women always told the truth in such situations. But they created the legal presumption anyway, because the consequences of the higher standard were unbearable.

Rav Mosheh did essentially the same thing. The situation in the USSR made false claims more likely, but it also made true claims impossible to prove. The balance of these changes meant that the rule should be left intact.

However, a compromise was available. Rav Mosheh had the option of telling the rabbi to try to verify the woman's claim before permitting her to remarry. Pitchei Teshuvah 17:158 cites RADBAZ as saying that in some cases where an investigation can be done easily, it must be done.

Rav Mosheh declines the compromise, on two grounds. First, he asserts that RADBAZ required investigation only in cases where a woman was reputed to be licentious, not as a general rule. (It seems likely that Rav Mosheh did not see the original of Shu"t Radbaz 3:542, which strongly confirms his position. Radbaz's case seems to be one in which the woman had previously made a false claim to be widowed.) Second, he writes that since there is a man prepared to marry the widow, and that man may not be willing to wait around while the rabbi investigates – the case is one of *iggun gamur*, absolute iggun, just as if the woman were being prevented from marrying anyone ever. (It's not clear whether Rav Mosheh would have the same objection if the woman had no beau in hand.)

I derive three principles from Rav Mosheh's responsum.

1.

While chazokohs are influenced by social changes, there is no straight line from a change in circumstances to a change in law. The legal presumptions that Chazal created via chazakot resulted from an interplay between their evaluation of reality and their sense of what halakhic outcomes were necessary or desirable. A competent posek must consider how changed circumstance affect the reality underlying the chazokoh and also whether allowing those changes to affect the chazokoh would yield undesirable halakhic outcomes.

2.

Decisions in agunah cases are not a choice between *chumra* (stringency) and *kulla* (leniency). Preventing a woman from remarrying is a wrong comparable to the stringency of allowing a woman to commit adultery.

I don't mean that 50/50 cases should be decided by a coinflip, or even necessarily that one can permit remarriage when the odds are less than 999,999,999 to 1. What I mean is that Chazal set up a very precise balance, and that any deviation from that balance, either way, is equally problematic.

3.

For agunot, justice delayed is justice denied.

Halakhists who are judged incompetent to issue new stringencies are unlikely to succeed in implementing new leniencies._

Chapter 3

CHANGING REALITIES AND NEW RABBINIC LEGISLATION

Imagine if a new technology enabled all 39 *melakhot* to be done on Shabbat without violating any existing halakhic prohibitions. How should our *poskim* respond?

Discussions of halakhic innovation often revolve around an asserted need for new leniencies. But it stands to reason that changed circumstances will require just as many new stringencies, and that the authority to make changes must apply both ways. If today's halakhists are judged incompetent to issue new stringencies, they are unlikely to succeed in implementing new leniencies.

Rabbinic *gezeirot* function to "build a protective fence"[1] around the Torah by forbidding actions that might lead to violations of Torah prohibitions. New circumstances yield new threats and require new *gezeirot*. However, in *Yabia Omer* 1:16, Rav Ovadiah Yosef zt"l writes that "It is well known that our teachers the rishonim and acharonim have stated broadly that we may not decree *gezeirot* based on our own judgment." Rav Ovadiah cites six sources to directly substantiate this principle.

My purpose here is to reopen the discussion, based on an analysis of those sources, and to compare Rav Ovadiah's approach with that of Rav Mosheh Feinstein zt"l.

Rav Ovadiah addresses the issue of whether to forbid reading by the light of an electric lamp on Shabbat.

Mishnah Shabbat 11a teaches that one may not read on Shabbat by the light of an oil lamp, although one may read by the light of a fireplace. Talmud Shabbat 12b explains that the concern is lest one violate the prohibition against kindling by tilting the lamp to improve its draw. This concern plainly does not apply to electric lamps. Therefore, the Mishnah's *gezeirah* does not apply to reading under electric lamps. However, because electric lamps can be turned off very easily, one can argue plausibly that reading by them **should** be forbidden, and that the Talmudic rabbis **would** have forbidden this had such lights existed in their time.

Rav Ovadiah's first source regarding the appropriateness of new *gezeirot* is a responsum of Rabbi Israel Bruna (*Shu"t Mahari Bruna* #108), one of the leading poskim of fifteenth-century Germany. Mahari Bruna discusses whether a woman who immerses while wearing a loose ring on her finger is permitted to resume intimacy with her husband. Immersion is valid only if the water can reach all the woman's skin, and the concern is that if we permit loose rings, women will come to wear tight rings that obstruct the water's access. He notes that Ramban and Rashba disagreed about whether *halakhah* requires removal of a loose ring in advance (*lekhatchilah*) of immersion, but he asserts that "after the fact (*bediavad*), no one disputes that from the day that the Talmud was sealed, no *gezeirah* was initiated that we do not find in the Talmud, as Rabbeinu Asher (Rosh) wrote in *Shabbat* Chapter 2 regarding the 'convulsion of the Geonim.'" Therefore, because the Talmud did not ban immersion with a loose ring, Mahari Bruna rules that the woman is permitted to resume intimacy with her husband.

I am puzzled by Rav Ovadiah's citation of this responsum with regard to electric lamps. A decree against reading by electric lamps declares that something should not be done; it does not invalidate something that has been done. It is therefore parallel to a decree against immersing while wearing a loose ring. Since Mahari Bruna is open to prohibiting women from immersing with loose rings, even though the Talmud did not, he should therefore also be open to prohibiting reading by electric light.

Mahari Bruna's distinction between an initial decree (*lekhathilah*) and invalidating a ritual after the fact (*bediavad*) also seems inconsistent with the Rosh he cites as support, which is also Rav Ovadiah's second source.

Rosh (to <u>Shabbat 2:15</u>) cites the Geonim as follows:
"We do not practice saying [a *berakhah* specific for fast days] in the evening [*amidah*], or even in the morning [*amidah*], lest he be seized

by illness or convulsion and eat something, making it turn out that he was a liar in his prayer."

Rosh responds:

"I am astonished: How could the Geonim initiate a *gezeirah* after Rav Ashi sealed the Talmud?!"

The issue here is *lekhathilah* – should one or shouldn't one say the *berakhah*? This is parallel to forbidding immersion while wearing a loose ring, and is *not* parallel to invalidating an immersion after the fact. The Geonim presumably did not decree that one who says the *berakhah* must repeat the *amidah*. I am therefore at a loss to explain why Mahari Bruna cites Rosh as supporting his claim that post-Talmudic rabbis are restricted only from making *bediavad* decrees.

Regardless, Rosh seems to support Rav Ovadiah's principle by stating an absolute rule against new decrees, albeit implicitly conceding that the Geonim rejected this rule. However, we can interpret Rosh's rule more narrowly. Rosh and Mahari Bruna both deal with decrees that apply to situations already considered by the Talmud. The question before them is whether to initiate a prohibition when, facing the same circumstances, the Rabbis of the Talmud chose not to prohibit. Rosh's rule may therefore be irrelevant to the issue of whether post-Talmudic authorities can make decrees in response to entirely new circumstances such as electric lamps.

This distinction between precedented and unprecedented circumstances emerges clearly from Rav Ovadiah's third source, Radbaz's commentary *Yikar Tiferet* to Rambam (*Hilkhot Terumot 1:22*). Radbaz discusses a dispute between Rambam and Raavad as to whether grains grown outside the Land of Israel become rabbinically obligated in *terumot* and *ma'asrot* when brought to Israel. Radbaz explains that Rambam held that "we should not initiate *gezeirot* based on our own judgment, since [such a decree] is not mentioned anywhere. Indeed, in the Yerushalmi they discussed this Mishnah at great length and never mentioned [the possibility] that [these grains] would be rabbinically obligated!" Radbaz explicitly frames Rambam's argument against such a decree in terms of acting where our predecessors chose not to.

Rav Ovadiah's fourth source, Maggid Mishneh (to *Hilkhot Hametz u-Matzah* 5:20), similarly addresses whether later rabbis can make new decrees when addressing the same circumstances as their predecessors. He understands Rambam as permitting the baking of *matzot* with oil or wine or honey added to the dough, because the combination does not rise faster than a dough with only water in it. Raavad limits this permission to *zerizim* (people eager to fulfill mitzvot punctiliously), but he forbids it to ordinary folks. Maggid Mishneh responds on behalf of Rambam: "But I say: We may not decree *gezeirot* based on our own judgment." People certainly considered baking with these additives in the time of the Talmud.

Similarly, Rav Ovadiah's fifth source, again from Radbaz (*Shu"t Radbaz* 1:149), also addresses a case of unchanged circumstances. Radbaz there considers whether a woman who experiences a *hargashah* (sensation associated with becoming *niddah*), but then inspects herself and finds no blood, should be considered a *niddah* under Rabbinic law. He responds that "we should not initiate *gezeirot* based on our own judgement in circumstances where our predecessors did not decree." The phenomenon of *hargashah* without finding blood of course also existed in Talmudic times.

Note that Radbaz and Maggid Mishneh each introduce the rule against new *gezeirot* to explain why Rambam permits where Raavad forbids. This suggests that Raavad (like the Geonim cited by Rosh above) may not agree with even our narrow understanding of the rule, and he might permit making new *gezeirot* even when circumstances have not changed significantly.[2]

However, Rav Ovadiah's sixth source, Rabbeinu Nissim (RAN, cited in *Shu"t HaRivash* #390), at first glance supports the claim that we cannot make new decrees even in response to new circumstances. RAN responds to a rabbi's request that he ban a community's practice of announcing real estate sales at Shabbat davening. These announcements served the public policy purpose of establishing a presumption of legitimate ownership (if no one came forward to contest the sale). This public good certainly suffices to override the general prohibition against speaking of business matters on Shabbat. RAN notes, however, that the Mishnah (*Beitzah 36b*) forbids *batei din* (halakhic courts) from adjudicating on Shabbat even in cases of public need, lest they come to write. Shouldn't the same consideration forbid this practice? RAN responds that we should not extend that prohibition to this case "because we only have those [*gezeirot*] listed by Chazal, and we should not originate *gezeirot* on our own." Here is a new practice, and yet RAN rules out making a new *gezeirah*.[3]

Yet the key phrase here is "those [*gezeirot*] **listed** by Chazal." To what list is RAN referring? Rabbinic literature contains no comprehensive list of *gezeirot* that we can check to see if it includes a decree against announcing real estate sales on Shabbat. Rather, RAN must be referring to the Mishnah in *Beitzah (36b)*, which includes a **list** of activities prohibited on Shabbat and Yom Tov despite their being "something of a mitzvah" (*reshut*),[4] among them the convening of a *beit din*. The Talmud (ibid 37a) identifies writing as the concern behind the prohibition. RAN explicitly classifies these announcements as *reshut*. His argument against banning these announcements is that the Mishnah intended its list to be exhaustive, and therefore with regard to the specific question of banning a *reshut* that might lead to writing, "we only have those [*gezeirot*] listed by Chazal." This argument has no relevance to a general rule against new decrees.

Thus, none of Rav Ovadiah's six sources explicitly supports a rule against initiating new *gezeirot* in unprecedented circumstances, and several of them implicitly acknowledge that the Geonim and Raavad allowed new *gezeirot* even in precedented circumstances.

Nevertheless, a broader restriction against new prohibitions may have developed after Radbaz. Such a development may be revealed in the many sources that Rav Ovadiah cites later in his responsum. Moreover, there may be practical reasons making such decrees impossible today. For example, making *gezeirot* might require a degree of public acknowledgement and deference that is not given to any contemporary halakhist or group of halakhists.

Rav Mosheh Feinstein (*Igrot Moshe OC 4:50*) also addresses the question of whether new *gezeirot* are possible in response to new

circumstances. His concern is not electric lamps, but rather the potential of electric timers to completely transform the Shabbat experience: "It is obviously forbidden to permit this, because via such timers one could do all the forbidden categories of labor on Shabbat, and [run] all factories, and there could be no greater devaluation of Shabbat."
Rav Moshe adds: "It's clear that had this device existed in the times of the Tannaim and Amoraim, they would have forbidden this."

Rav Moshe is less certain "that we cannot forbid what the Sages did not forbid, and that one may not derive further prohibitions from their decrees, even against things that are rationally more stringent." Even if we cannot, he insists that anything not prohibited by Chazal, "even though this was because the case didn't exist in their time, and thus there is no actual prohibition, nonetheless one should not permit it, since it is something that it would be appropriate to forbid." The circumlocutions in this responsum are striking and astonishing: "forbidden to permit," "appropriate to forbid," and so forth. Clearly, Rav Moshe felt that something goes seriously awry when *halakhah* cannot effectively rebuild its fences in response to new circumstances.[5]

The authority to issue new permissions or create new obligations is not necessarily subject to the same rules as the authority to forbid. One can construct a theoretical system[6] that gives contemporary halakhists the authority to make new decrees freeing *agunot* without simultaneously enabling them to ban putting televisions on Shabbat timers. Maybe that authority could also enable regulating publicly owned corporations and responding effectively to the existence of a Jewish state.

But it seems far more intuitive to connect the issues practically, and even to claim that permitting what would otherwise be forbidden requires more authority than forbidding what would otherwise be permitted. Therefore, advocates for creative halakhic legislation should recognize that the authority to issue new decrees will almost certainly go both ways, and that generating the authority to permit may require granting the authority to forbid. My hope is that this essay opens space for serious discussion of the extent to which we wish to grant that authority.

[1] See, e.g., *Mishnah Avot* 1:1.

[2] Raavad generally sees himself as continuing Geonic tradition, so this historical conjunction would not be surprising.

[3] Real estate sales existed in the time of Hazal, and therefore one might argue that here as well Hazal **chose** not to ban announcing them, so Ran also is not relevant to the question of new technologies. But since the practice of announcing them did not exist, this seems to me an overreach.

[4] The Mishnah uses the term *reshut*, which Rashi here defines as *ketzat mitzvah* ("something of a mitzvah").

[5] The validity of Rav Moshe's discomfort is independent of the question of whether one shares his intuition about the negative implications of timers for the Shabbat experience.

[6] For example, by distinguishing between *gezeirot* and *takkanot*.

Every person's best interest in every situation is to serve G-d and act in accordance with His will. If the best interests of two people appear to conflict, must one of them have gotten His will wrong?

Chapter 4

CAN THERE BE A CONFLICT OF INTEREST AMONG MORAL PERSONS?

One of my all-time favorite books is Benjamin Freedman z"l's <u>Duty and Healing</u>. Among its many virtues is a clear presentation of how ethical conversations grounded in duty can be more productive than conversations grounded in rights. In a rights-based model, the parties have conflicting interests. The question is who "gets" to make the decision. In a duty-based model, everyone's shared interest is that the best decision be made. Opinions may conflict but not interests.

Freedman adopts the conventional tack of identifying the halakhic system as duty-based and Western ethics as rights-based. But the strongest formulation I know of the advantage he claims for duty based systems is found in the quintessentially American philosopher Ayn Rand. She declared that "**There is no conflict of interests among men**, neither in business nor in trade nor in their most personal desires—if they omit the irrational from their view of the possible and destruction from their view of the practical".

Let us concede that the irrational is rarely banished successfully (and perhaps should not be), and that destruction is often regarded as a viable option. In practice, therefore, even the most rational of people often believe their interests to be opposed. But the underlying premise seems sound within halakhah. Every person's best or true interest in every situation is to do their duty, to serve G-d and act in accordance with His will.

It therefore seems worth asking to what extent halakhic reasoning can tolerate a claim that the ultimate interests of human beings are genuinely opposed. Can two people genuinely acting in accordance with His will find their moral interests in conflict?

As an illustration: When two people each lay claim to an abandoned toga, their economic interests are certainly in conflict. Furthermore, A may believe that she grabbed the toga first, and B may believe that he grabbed it first. But they share the moral interest of ensuring that the property is given to its true owner, and if that is unknowable, they share the moral interest of upholding the ruling of the court that it be split. Conflict should occur only when people mistake their true interests,

I grant that in some extreme cases a halakhic court may withdraw and declare *kol d'alim gvar* = whoever is stronger, i.e. that whoever successfully seizes the property as a matter of fact will be recognized as the owner by law. But this does not affect my argument. In such cases, either there are no moral interests – if one can religiously accept that some human decisions are a matter of entire indifference to G-d - or else the moral interests are unrelated to ownership, but rather to questions such as who has greater need of the property, or would use it best. (Deborah Klapper asks why the court allows a contest of force rather than directly granting the property to one part on moral grounds, which is a possible understanding of *shuda dedaini*, another mechanism used in such cases. But determining which mechanism is used when, and why, is beyond the scope of this essay.)

A more challenging case may arise out of the narrative that concludes Parshat Balak. Explicating that challenge requires an extended halakhic excursus.

Pinchas is outraged when Zimri, *nasi* of the tribe of Shim'on, publicly flaunts his dalliance with Kozbi bat Tzur, daughter of the *nasi* of Midyan. He steps forward and fatally skewers the two sinners. Mishnah Sanhedrin justifies his action under the rubric *kannoin pog'in bo* (*kannoin*/zealots may execute people committing this sin). Vigilante justice is legitimated in such cases even though the sin is not a capital crime under the Torah's formal regime of criminal law. (Note: The very existence of such a category is profoundly dangerous, and there is absolute halakhic consensus that it has no contemporary relevance. The legal analysis below is engaged in solely to address the philosophic question above.)

Talmud Sanhedrin 82a provides the following analysis:

אמר רב חסדא:
הבא לימלך - אין מורין לו . . .
ולא עוד, אלא
שאם פירש זמרי והרגו פנחס –
נהרג עליו;
נהפך זמרי והרגו לפנחס –
אין נהרג עליו,
שהרי רודף הוא

Said Rav Chisda:

If someone comes to ask (whether they may play the vigilante) – they may not rule for him . . .

Not only this, but

if Zimri had separated from Kazbi, and Pinchas had nonetheless killed him –

Pinchas would be executed for killing him;

if Zimri had turned about and killed Pinchas –

Zimri would not be executed for killing him,

because after all Pinchas is a *rodef* (pursuer).

(Note: The Talmud does not address Kazbi's rights and obligations, and that discussion is beyond the scope of this essay.)

Rav Chisda makes clear that the legitimate vigilante exists in a halakhic twilight zone. He or she is apparently acting in accordance with the Torah, yet halakhists must not affirm this to them even when they ask. Furthermore, the *kannoi's* legitimate target is nonetheless entitled to regard them as a pursuer and to fight back and even kill them in self-defense, just as they can any other *rodef.*

In addition to the right and duty of self-defense against deadly attackers, the law of *rodef* includes a duty for bystanders to intervene on the side of the *nirdaf* (pursued) against the *rodef.* Commentators ask the logical next question: Do third parties have a duty to intervene against the *kannoi?* The consensus answer is no. But that answer begs the practical question. Since the vigilante is not acting on the basis of a ruling, third parties cannot know that he or she is anything other than an ordinary murderer, and should therefore have a duty to intervene.

A possible answer is that third parties can act only on the basis of certainty. Where the apparent victim is actively engaged in a relevant transgression, such certainty is impossible, since the apparent pursuer might be a legitimate zealot. The right of self-defense does not require the same degree of certainty. Therefore, the victim may or must self-defend even though bystanders may not intervene.

Mishneh l'Melekh challenges the Talmud's ruling as self-contradictory. "If Zimri had separated from Kazbi, and Pinchas had nonetheless killed him – Pinchas would be executed for killing him" means that the *kannoi's* action is legitimate only while the transgression is ongoing. But the law of the *rodef* authorizes deadly force only **when necessary** to remove the threat. Why may Zimri kill Pinchas as a *rodef* when he can remove the threat simply by ceasing to sin?!

This question can be resolved formally in at least three ways.

1. One can argue that the Talmud does not justify Zimri's lethal self-defense but rather exempts him from capital punishment. The unnecessary use of deadly force against pursuers is a crime, but not a capital crime. Thus Zimri in fact was obligated to save himself by ceasing to sin instead of killing Pinchas. (This approach generates literature about whether it is inherently not a capital crime, or rather that there are insurmountable evidentiary barriers to capital prosecution.)

2. One can argue that the proper formulation of the law of rodef is not "use deadly force only when necessary", but rather "use only the degree of force necessary". This formulation means that the threat of violence cannot compel a person to hide, or to cease their otherwise chosen activities, even if those activities are illegal. (This raises the question of whether an ordinary murderer retains the right of self-defense against interveners. Again, the consensus answer is no. The simplest formal response is that that halakhah automatically deputizes third parties in such cases, and the right of self-defense does not apply against officers of the courts acting in the legitimate course of their duties.)

3. One can argue that halakhah defines withdrawal-while-erect as a sexual act, so that in the moment of Pinchas' attack, Zimri had no practical way of ceasing to sin. This approach is advanced by the author of Chelkat Yoav in the anthology Degel HaTorah, at the end of Siman 13.

Under Chelkat Yoav's approach, it seems to me that Zimri was not only permitted but actually obligated to kill Pinchas.

Chelkat Yoav generalizes his argument to other cases in which the Torah permits but does not obligate killing. Thus the Talmud records a dispute whether the *goeil hadam* = blood-avenger (another case with no contemporary relevance) is permitted or obligated to kill the *rotzeiach b'shogeg* = accidental murderer. Chelkat Yoav argues that according to the position that the blood-avenger is only permitted to kill, the accidental murderer has a right – I contend duty – of self-defense against the blood-avenger.

Now this does not yet generate a conflict of moral interests, because one can argue that the *goeil hadam* is permitted but **ought not** to kill the *rotzeiach b'shogeg*. This may follow from the Torah's description of the *goeil hadam* as acting in the grip of overwhelming emotion. So everyone's moral interest is that the *rotzeiach b'shogeg* not be killed.

However, Rambam (Issurei Biah 12:4-5) states clearly that the *kannoi* is praiseworthy, just before recording Zimri's right of self-defense.

It follows that under Chelkat Yoav's approach, Pinchas **ought to** try his best to kill Zimri, and Zimri **ought to** try his best to prevent Pinchas from killing him. This is an opposition not merely of practical but of moral interests, and is not generated by any difference in the information available to the parties.

One can escape this conclusion by rejecting the implication I drew from Chelkat Yoav; by rejecting Chelkat Yoav's approach; by rejecting Rambam's praise of the *kannoi*; and in many other ways. The question I am asking is whether it is religiously necessary to escape this conclusion because halakhic Judaism cannot countenance having moral interests conflict.

Probability and law have a fraught relationship.

Chapter 5

HALAKHAH AND REALITY DON'T ALWAYS HAVE TO AGREE

Jackie Mason observed that when there's a fifty percent chance of rain, half an umbrella won't keep you dry. Having a whole umbrella half the time is also not a sensible response. Probability and reality don't always interact smoothly.

For that matter, what are the odds that probability is usefully predictive? This sort of puzzle twists some of us into epistemological pretzels. Our friends wonder why we care, since they're one hundred percent sure that it is in fact predictive in our reality. Great mathematicians, physicists, and fantasy writers wonder what it would be like to live in a different reality.

Also Talmudists. On Chullin 11a, the Talmud asks: "From whence cometh that thing the rabbis say: *"zil batar ruba"* = "Follow the majority"? The question doesn't relate to the context of voting, the Talmud clarifies; nor to bounded sets, such as which of 32 ping-pong balls will emerge first from a cage. Such cases derive from the verse *"acharei rabom l'hatot"* (=*after the plurality to incline*). The question relates to predicting the future on the basis of past experience. For example: Can we assume that minors will become fertile adults?

Most of the practical consequences provided by the Talmud are esoteric. On Yebamot 61a, Rabbi Meir is cited as holding that prepubescents are forbidden to engage in either *yibum* (levirate marriage) or *chalitzah* (rejection of levirate marriage). He has a verse to prove *chalitzah*, but none for *yibum*. Why then forbid *yibum*? Because *yibum* becomes incest if either party grows up to be sterile (as defined by halakhah). Rabbi Meir's colleagues dismiss this concern on the grounds that most adults are not sterile, and therefore most minors will not be sterile as adults. The Talmud generalizes this dispute. Rabbi Meir consistently "is concerned for the minority", whereas the Rabbis are not, saying "*zil batar ruba*". What justifies the Rabbis?

A host of Amoraim suggest sources. Their shared approach is to find a Torah law that could never be implemented if not for "*zil batar ruba*". For example: the Torah forbids us not to break any of the Pesach sacrifice's bones even after it is slaughtered. Yet a sacrifice is invalid and may not be eaten if the brain membrane was punctured, and the only way to know for certain whether it was intact is to fracture the skull and look! Or: How can the Torah establish penalties for incest, when paternity cannot be proven? (Here the Talmudic imagination faltered. No one suggested that the law would become enforceable in the future, after the discovery of DNA.)

Rav Ashi is the last to suggest a source. We eat meat even though an animal with a punctured trachea or esophagus is not kosher. How can we know for certain that the slaughterer's knife did not erase all evidence of such a puncture?

Rav Ashi proudly presents this source to Rav Kehana, who upends everything. Maybe we rely on probability **only when we have no choice**? And maybe even Rabbi Meir agrees that we rely on probability when absolutely necessary, for example in order to eat meat. Even if Rabbi Meir was vegetarian, surely he agreed that it was possible and necessary to fulfill the command of eating from the Passover sacrifice! The upshot seems to be that where halakhah cannot function without accepting probability, we don't need a source to justify using it. Sources are needed only where probability is a convenience or luxury.

The 13th century commentator RASHBA (Rabbi Shlomoh ben Aderet) challenges the Talmud's claim of necessity. We all agree that the animal's trachea and esophagus may **or may not** have been punctured before slaughter. Why can't we reject probability and still eat meat on the ground that it might not have been punctured? Why not say that everything is permitted unless it is certainly prohibited?

RASHBA's answer is to introduce a second rule: The Torah itself forbids us to perform actions that might or might not be forbidden, unless they are **more likely** permitted than not.

By contrast, RAMBAM held that the Torah **permits** us to perform actions that might or might not be forbidden, unless they are **more likely forbidden** than not. It is the Rabbis who forbade such actions unless they are more likely permitted; or in many cases, much more likely permitted, or in some cases, much, much more likely permitted. RASHBA argues that if RAMBAM is correct, the Talmud's proofs fail.

The basis of RASHBA's argument seems to be that if we reject probability, **everything possible must be treated as equally likely.** So every piece of meat might or might not be from an animal whose trachea was punctured before slaughter; every sexual partner might or might not be your sibling. But why should it be forbidden to eat a Passover sacrifice just because it **might** not be kosher, when it might be kosher?

RASHBA's attack on RAMBAM is therefore really an attack on the Talmud's apparent assumption that the default is prohibition, and that probability is necessary to permit cases that are in any way ambiguous. Let's say instead that everything is permitted until it is absolutely, demonstrably, one hundred percent forbidden!

There are areas of halakhah where this may be the case. For example: on the Biblical level, Rav Mosheh Feinstein understood this to be the rule about *mamzerut*, and on the Rabbinic level, Rav Shimon Shkop may understand this to be the case about *orlah* (fruit produced in a tree's first three years) outside the Land of Israel.

However, Rav Shkop finds Rambam's apparent position intolerable on different grounds than RASHBA. How could the Torah leave it acceptable to take spiritual chances, to trust to the odds when it comes to the safety of one's soul?

Rav Shkop draws the analogy to physical safety. Yoma 84b and Ketubot 16b record Rav Yehuda quoting Rav stating that we must act to save a life regardless of the odds, even if that entails violating Shabbat; it follows that we cannot act in ways that put a life at risk. Shouldn't it be at least as prohibited to put a soul at risk? Shulkhan Arukh OC 306:14 in fact rules that one must violate Shabbat to save someone from apostasizing, i.e to save an at-risk soul.

We can quibble with the analogy. Perhaps committing a single sin is not quite risking one's spiritual life, though who is to say which sins are deadly and which merely flesh wounds? Halakhah permits taking reasonable physical risks to earning a living and to participate in what one's society considers normal life. Perhaps that is also true with regard to spiritual risks.

But Rav Shkop's underlying point stands. In most circumstances, Torah doesn't permit eating foods that probably aren't deadly poisons, but might be, so why would it permit meat that probably isn't *treif*, but might be?

R. Shkop's fascinating solution for Rambam is that the Torah doesn'tdoesn't need to prohibit taking such risks; we will naturally avoid them in the same way that we avoid pointless physical risks.[1]

R. Shkop then says something much more radical. He suggests that even according to Rambam, the Torah prohibits actions that might be sinful. But the Torah gave halakhists the discretion to define "might". He draws the analogy to explanations that give the Rabbis discretion over which forms of labor are Biblically prohibited on Chol Hamoed, or which forms of "affliction" are Biblically mandated on Yom Kippur, and in general to the mechanism of "*mesaran hakatuv lachakhamim*", roughly "Scripture delegated its authority to the Sages".

This position is at least compatible with the idea that every possibility is equally likely, and probability is a human imposition on the world. In this reading, our Talmud passage is not asking where the Rabbis derived *zil batar ruba* from, but rather how we know that they derived it. The answer is: We can know this because they never banned

---

[11] (Here I need to express my appreciation for Rabbi Alex Ozar's marvelously clear article "These are matters that shatter roofs": R. Shimon Shkop on Law and Normativity More Broadly" (Dinei Yisrael vol. 20), which sent me running to R. Shkop's Shaarei Yosher. R. Ozar argues that R. Shkop sees avoidance of spiritual risk as an ought, not merely an is, even according to Rambam, even though it is not a formal halakhic obligation. I hope to engage more fully with that understanding in a future installment. For now, I note only that halakhah certainly prohibits taking excessive physical risk, with "excessive" coming into play long before the odds of death and life are even. Former Soviet Roulette is forbidden, period.)

eating meat, or declared the mitzvah of eating the Passover sacrifice to be purely hypothetical.

Another way of thinking about it is this: every possibility exists. There are universes where the animal is kosher, and universes where its esophagus really was punctured just where the knife went through.

Or maybe these universes exist only until halakhah chooses. But here, halakhah delegates its authority to halakhists. When they decide that we can rely on the odds that the food is kosher, it really is kosher, because they make our world one where the animal's throat was whole.

The problem is that reality sometimes bites; we find out that we were wrong. Unknown to us, X-rays at the Pesach sacrifice's last checkup revealed a hole in the esophagus. How can this be, if our Torah choices determined that there was no hole?

Maybe the Rabbis chose not to fully determine reality, to allow themselves to be wrong on occasion. Follow them, and you will live in a matching universe **almost** every time. But not every time.

Why would the rabbis choose that way? Because if following the rules always works, it becomes too easy to think that the point of living is to follow the rules, like paint-by-numbers artists perfectly painting within the lines without ever seeing the overall picture. A truly perfect halakhah would make us think of moral development as superfluous.

Deborah Klapper suggests a different reason. Not everything is probabilistic; sometimes reality just is. If halakhah and reality always corresponded in probabilistic cases, we might mistakenly conclude that they always corresponded, period, and refuse to correct even the most egregious halakhic errors of fact.

PART II

EQUALITY AS A TORAH VALUE

"the laws of the government and of the state obligate the citizens and have force only if they are democratic with no distinction at all among citizens"

Chapter 6

EQUAL PROTECTION OF THE LAWS

The 14th Amendment to the United States Constitution declares that the relevant government authorities may not "deny to any person within its jurisdiction the equal protection of the laws." The commitment stated in this post-Civil War amendment is now seen as a restatement of the fundamental American ethic. Unequal laws are unjust per se. They also undermine democracy by entrenching power in those the law privileges and denying it to those the law disfavors.

The Torah states a similar ethic in at least four places:

Shemot 12:49

תּוֹרָה אַחַת
יִהְיֶה לָאֶזְרָח
וְלַגֵּר הַגָּר בְּתוֹכְכֶם

There must be one torah
for the ezrach
and for the ger *who is* gar *in your midst*

Vayikra 24:22

מִשְׁפַּט אֶחָד יִהְיֶה לָכֶם
כַּגֵּר כָּאֶזְרָח יִהְיֶה
כִּי אֲנִי יְקֹוָק אֱל-הֵיכֶם

There must be one mishpat *for you –*
the ger *and the* ezrach *must be alike*
because I am Hashem your G-d.

Bamidbar 9:14

חֻקָּה אַחַת יִהְיֶה לָכֶם
וְלַגֵּר וּלְאֶזְרַח הָאָרֶץ

there must be one chukah *for you*
and for the ger *and for the* ezrach *of the land*

Bamidbar 15:15-16

הַקָּהָ֗ל
חֻקָּ֤ה אַחַת֙ לָכֶ֣ם וְלַגֵּ֣ר הַגָּ֔ר
חֻקַּ֥ת עוֹלָ֖ם לְדֹרֹתֵיכֶ֑ם
כָּכֶ֛ם כַּגֵּ֥ר יִהְיֶ֖ה לִפְנֵ֥י יְקֹוָֽק׃
תּוֹרָ֥ה אַחַ֛ת וּמִשְׁפָּ֥ט אֶחָ֖ד יִהְיֶ֣ה לָכֶ֑ם וְלַגֵּ֖ר הַגָּ֥ר אִתְּכֶֽם׃

The kahal –
one chukah *for you and for the* ger *who is* gar;
It is an eternal chukah *for all your generations;*
you and the ger *must be alike before G-d.*

At least two mid-20th century scholars understand these verses as
generating a halakhic promise of equal protection in the context of the
principle that *dina demalkhuta dina* = the law of the government is the
law.

Rav Chaim Regensburg, Rosh Yeshiva of HTC and Av Beit Din of
Chicago, wrote in his article "Iyyunim al Zekhuyot Ezrachiyot" that

מכל זה נוכחנו
שכלל גדול הוא במשפטים ובחוקים שבמדינה
שצריך להיות שוויון מוחלט בין כל התושבים והאזרחים,
"חֻקָּ֤ה אַחַת֙ יִהְיֶ֣ה לָכֶ֔ם וְלַגֵּ֖ר וּלְאֶזְרַ֥ח הָאָֽרֶץ"
היא אחת התכונות העיקריות של כל חוק ומשפט
וחוק המשולל תכונה זו אינו חוק צדק
From all this we have proven
that it is a great principle of the chukim and mishpatim of a state
that there must be absolute equality among all
the toshavim and ezrachim.
"There must be one chukah for you
and for the ger and for the ezrach of the land"
is one of the essential characteristics of every chok and mishpat,
and a chok which lacks this characteristic is not a just chok.

Rav Efraim Fischel Weinberger of Tel Aviv wrote in his article
"*Samkhut Hatzibbur Bivchirat Anshei Hamemshal L'Or Hahalakhah*"
that

חק התורה
הוא נגד יצירת תחומים, הפליות
ומעמדים שונים בעלי זכויות יתר
"כלל התורה הוא: "חוקה אחת יהיה לכם"

. . .

יוצא איפוא
שחוקי המלכות והמדינה
מחייבים את האזרחים ויש להם תוקף
רק אם הם חוקים דמוקרטיים
בלי כל הבדל כל שהיא בין אזרח לאזרח ...
The chok of the Torah
is against the creation of boundaries, discriminations,
and classes with greater privileges.
The general principle of Torah is: "there must be one chukah for you"

...

It therefore emerges
that the chukim of the government and of the state
obligate the citizens and have force
only if they are democratic chukim
with no distinction at all among citizens ...

The claim that Halakhah mandates equal protection in the context of dina demalkhuta can be challenged in at least three ways. First, the halakhah of dina demalkhuta was articulated and maintained for a millennium in environments where the civil law discriminated against Jews. Second, Halakhah itself discriminates in various contexts between citizens (Jews) and resident aliens who are not Jewish, and even imposes some restrictions on naturalized citizens (converts). Third, Halakhah discriminates even among citizens in various contexts, for example on grounds of gender or lineage.

I'll briefly sketch two responses to the last two challenges, and a difficulty with each. But my focus is on the first challenge, and on a response to it that may be useful overall.

Response #1 – Equal protection applies specifically in the realm of dina demalkhuta, meaning laws developed via human reason. Divine laws need not meet the same standard.

The problem here is that the relevant Biblical verses relate to halakhah itself, and the diverse terminology (*torah, chok, mishpat*) suggests that they apply across all types of halakhah.

Response #2 – "Equal" does not mean "identical." According to https://constitutioncenter.org/interactive-constitution/interpretation/amendment-xiv/clauses/702, "most laws are assessed under so-called 'rational basis scrutiny.' Here, any plausible and legitimate reason for the discrimination is sufficient to render it constitutional." However, "laws that rely on so-called 'suspect classifications' are assessed under heightened scrutiny. Here, the government must have important or compelling reasons to justify the discrimination, and the discrimination must be carefully tailored to serve those reasons." Within halakhah, we need to determine what constitutes a "rational basis" for discrimination; and whether halakhah has the equivalent of "suspect classifications."

The problem here is figuring out what to do if existing laws seem not to meet the equal protection standard.

Moving back to the first challenge: A medieval halakhic consensus, beginning at least from Rabbi Yosef Ibn Migash among Sefardim (see his commentary to Bava Batra 55a) and perhaps from Rabbeinu Tam among Ashkenazim (see e.g. Talmidei Rabbeinu Peretz Nedarim 28a), held that *dina demalkhuta dina* applied only to laws that are כלליים/general rather than aimed at specific individuals, and that the government must be משוה מדותיו/relate to all equally. Rabbeinu Tam in some versions even bans laws that treat one מדינה /state within an empire differently from its peers. On this basis, Dr. Shmuel Shiloh in his excellent book Dina D'Malkhuta Dina, p. 110, asserts that

ברור,
שכאשר מדובר בחוק השווה לכל נפש,
הכוונה היא שהוא חל באופן שווה אף על היהודים.

It is clear
that when speaking of a *chok* that applies equally to all souls,
that the intent is that it applies in an equal manner even to Jews.

Dr, Shiloh's statement is in conscious opposition to the late 15th century <u>Rabbi Yosef Kolon</u>, who wrote (Responsa Maharik 194):

וגם אין לומר דהב' לא שייך למימר ד"ד
כיון שהישראל פורע יותר מהבותי,
שהרי כת' המרדכי שם
דלא אמרינן אלא כשהמלך משוה מדותיו
.דודאי פשיט' דשפיר מקרי משוה מדותיו
כיון שכל יהודי פורע בשוה דבר קצוב

One cannot say that *dina demalkhuta* does not apply here
because the Jew pays more than the nonJew,
because the Mordekhai wrote there that
"we say it only when the king relates to all equally,"
because it's obvious that "relates to all equally" is met
when all Jews pay an equal fixed amount.

Dr. Shiloh concedes that

למרות ריבוי המקומות השנים בעיקרון השוויון,
נאמר דבר זה במפורש במקום אחד לבד:
בסיום אחת מתשובותיו בתנ הריטב"א כך:
"והסכמת שופטי המלך בזה אינו מעלה כלום
אלא א"כ הוא חוק קבוע מן המלכו'
על **כל** המלכות
ואפי' על היהודיים
דקי"ל דינא דמלכותא דינא.

despite the many places that teach the root principle of equality,
this matter is stated explicitly in only one place.
At the end of one of his responsa (#53), Ritva writes:
"the consensus of the king's judges in this matter is of no avail
unless it is a *chok* that is established by the government
over the entire kingdom,
even on the Jews,
because we hold *dina demalkhuta dina*."

Dr. Shiloh understands this as a statement that *dina demalkhuta dina* applies only to laws that apply equally to Jews and nonJews. In my humble opinion, this is incorrect. The clause preceding Dr. Shiloh's quote is

למדנו מזה

שדברים אלו הם כפי המנהג

we have learned from this
that in these matters (the law) follows the practice.

Therefore, Ritva contends, the practice of non-Jewish courts is irrelevant to Jewish courts, unless the government has established this as a law that is binding even on Jews. The point is not that the law must apply equally to Jews – rather, the point is that there must be a law that applies to Jews, and not merely a convention of the state's non-Jewish judicial system. Otherwise rabbinic courts are free to follow their own conventions.

Maharik's position is brought by Rav Yosef Caro in Beit Yosef (Choshen Mishpat 369), but not in his Shulchan Arukh, while Rav Mosheh Isserles cites it in a gloss. So this issue may be a dispute between them as well.

What interests me is that Maharik and Dr. Shiloh each see their opposing positions as obvious despite a lack of explicit textual precedent. And I think they are both obviously correct! Maharik seems to me obviously correct historically that the Jewish community enforced taxes on themselves that were levied unequally. Dr. Shiloh seems to me obviously correct that this violates the fundamental consensus principle that law must be applied equally.

Rav Yekutiel Cohen, Av Beit Din of Ashdod, explains Maharik via Rav Shlomo Kluger's comment (Chokhmat Shlomo to Choshen Mishpat 369:8, available on Al HaTorah) that the equality standard applies only to citizens, not to resident aliens. Maharik assumed that Jews would always be considered aliens rather than citizens in non-Jewish polities. (Dr. Shiloh presumably rejects that assumption.)

According to Rav Kluger, we must say that the *ger* referred to in our equality verses is the convert, not the resident alien. But is it consistent with the spirit of these verses to discriminate against resident aliens without a rational basis for doing so?

Rabbi Cohen argues that there is a rational basis for such discrimination: alien minorities are often hated by the natives and require additional government services. Similarly, Ramban to Shemot 1:10 records that Pharaoh began his campaign against the Jews by imposing a labor levy on us, "because it is the way of *gerim* in the land to offer a labor levy to the king." Not coincidentally, Ramban limits the authority of *dina demalkhuta dina* to regulations that fall within the conventional practice of kings.

However, Responsa Ateret Paz (1:3 CM 4) puts Ramban's explanation in a different context. After imposing the labor levy, Pharaoh escalates by asking the midwives to kill all Jewish male infants at birth. When they refuse, Pharaoh cites Maharik's position that *dina demalkhuta* applies even to discriminatory laws! The midwives reply that it applies only to laws that meet the equality standard.

In other words, the legitimation of discrimination (sometimes? often? always?) leads to its expansion. But protests are more often effective when they reflect a moral consensus than when they oppose it. Perhaps the Jews could have successfully refused the labor levy, as the midwives refused the order to murder. Or perhaps disobeying what was seen as a legitimate tax would have turned all Egypt against them faster – in fact, Ramban suggests that popular outrage forced Pharaoh to cancel his general decree against male Jewish infants after only three months.

It seems to me that the equality standard functions in halakhah as an aspirational ideal. It is implemented only when doing so will not destabilize the rule of law, or alternatively, when it is violated so grossly that revolution is both justified and very likely to succeed.

Jews in the United States are blessed with full citizenship in a country that shares our moral aspiration of having the law provide equal protection to all human beings. The meaning of equal protection is not always clear, and reasonable people can disagree about the risk/benefit ratio of various forms of activism. But there should be no doubt of our

Torah obligation to work toward the realization of this Torah aspiration.

My thanks to all those who participated in the CMTL Yom Iyyun on Dr. Martin Luther King Jr. Day 2019. They helped sharpen several of the ideas in this essay, although the work is far from complete.

Rav Yaakov Kaminetsky held that the possibility of conversion rescues Judaism from the charge of racism

Chapter 7

Equality and Chosenness

At a public conference thirty years ago, a prominent Jewish intellectual explained to great acclaim why he no longer accepted the idea that Jews are "chosen." His argument was as follows. All human beings are created *b'tzelem Elokim*; therefore, each human being is infinitely valuable; therefore, each human being is equally valuable.

I raised my hand. Mathematicians, I asked, disagree[2] about whether all infinities are equal. Would you have a moral problem with someone claiming that chosenness creates a "larger infinity?"

No one else present was interested in my question. In any case, I myself am deeply committed to the absolute ontological equality of all human beings. I recognize that distinguishing among infinities is dangerously similar to an Orwellian declaration that "Some people are more equal than others." I follow Rav Yaakov Kaminetsky z"l's argument in his commentary to Avot that Judaism would be irredeemably racist if not for the possibility of conversion, and therefore "chosenness" must relate to a responsibility that can be voluntarily assumed by nonJews. (Rabbi Kaminetsky plainly excluded any understanding of conversion as effecting a miraculous ontological shift.)

Nonetheless, the distinction inherent in my question matters. There is a moral gulf between those who assume the infinite value of each human being, and build particularist pride atop that foundation, and those who build pride by diminishing others.

I have seen both in Jewish contexts. During my year in Israel, a rabbi at an affiliated institution – a man with many admirable traits – regularly gave allegedly inspirational lectures filled with comments that diminished the humanity of nonJews. These lectures seemed to me to

---

[2] Various mathy friends inform me that the issue has been settled now.

have an almost visibly corrosive impact on the souls of his students. But I also acknowledge that some Chabad shluchim strike me as superb examples of treating each human being as infinitely valuable without compromising on their belief in Jewish superiority. The world would be a much better place if everyone cared for each other on quotidian matters the way those shluchim care for nonJews.

This issue arose for me this week in the context of Netziv's explanation of *naaseh v'nishma*.

In Shemot 24:3, we read:

וַיָּבֹא מֹשֶׁה וַיְסַפֵּר לָעָם
אֵת כָּל־דִּבְרֵי יְקֹוָק וְאֵת כָּל־הַמִּשְׁפָּטִים
וַיַּעַן כָּל־הָעָם קוֹל אֶחָד וַיֹּאמְרוּ
כָּל־הַדְּבָרִים אֲשֶׁר־דִּבֶּר יְקֹוָק נַעֲשֶׂה:

Mosheh came and recounted to the nation
all of Hashem's words and all the regulations.
The entire nation responded in one voice, saying:
All the words that Hashem spoke – we will do (= naaseh).

Four verses later, we read

וַיִּקַּח סֵפֶר הַבְּרִית
וַיִּקְרָא בְּאָזְנֵי הָעָם
וַיֹּאמְרוּ
כָּל אֲשֶׁר־דִּבֶּר יְקֹוָק נַעֲשֶׂה וְנִשְׁמָע:

(Mosheh) took the scroll of the covenant
and read/proclaimed (it) in the ears of the nation.
They said:
All that Hashem spoke – we will do and we will heed (=naaseh
venishma)

Netziv raises three questions. First, if the Jews had already committed to doing "All the words that Hashem spoke," what was Mosheh seeking to accomplish by reading the "scroll of the covenant" to them? Second, why is only the first response attributed to "the entire nation?" Third, what does "we will heed" add to "we will do?"

Grouping the questions makes clear that the overall structure of the answer will be: Mosheh read the scroll of the covenant so that some (but not all) of the nation would add "we will heed" to "we will do."

Netziv formulates the distinction between "doing" and "heeding" as follows: "Doing" means performing the actions that G-d commands, but "heeding" means performing them **with the intention** that G-d commands. Netziv believes that the intention that G-d commands is that one perform them entirely for His sake, rather than because they accord with nature or human reason.

Netziv constructs the following timeline. In the Ten Commandments and immediate aftermath, G-d makes clear to the Jews that he insists on their studying Torah and engaging in worship (*torah va'avodah*), but he does not mention *gemilut chasadim*, the third pillar holding up the world. Why?

שהרי בטבעם
המה בני אברהם יצחק ויעקב
גומלי חסדים
Because by their nature
they are children of Avraham, Yitzchak, and Yaakov,
practitioners of chasadim

Because *chesed* was natural to them, when the Jews respond "All the words that Hashem spoke – we will do," they cannot be referring to *chesed*, because they would have done *chessed* even without the Divine command. Mosheh then reads to them the "Scroll of the Covenant," which Netziv identifies with Genesis, to explain that the Three Forefathers performed *chessed* for G-d's sake, and not just by nature. The elite of the nation understood the point and responded "We will do **and we will heed**" to emphasize their acceptance of the requirement for motivation.

I am not comfortable reading elite/mass distinctions into the narrative here (although I must acknowledge that Netziv is far from alone in doing so). I find it frankly disturbing that he understands "*naaseh venishma*" as reflecting the attitude of only the elite. But my

48

interest this week is his apparent claim that Jews are genetically more predisposed to *chessed* than are nonJews.

This is the kind of claim that can easily be turned to evil. *Chessed* is natural to Jews, but not to nonJews; therefore nonJews do not share at least one of G-d's thirteen attributes; therefore they are not truly created *b'tzelem Elokim*; and so on.

Which is why it is so absolutely vital that Netziv notices the danger and moves to preclude it. Even though his textual interpretation here in no way depends on any claim regarding nonJews, he adds in a sentence:

שהרי בטבעם
המה בני אברהם יצחק ויעקב
גומלי חסדים
וגם כל האוה"ע
על חסד נבנית העולם
Because by their nature
they are children of Avraham, Yitzchak, and Yaakov,
practitioners of chasadim
and so also are all the nations of the world
because the world was built (by G-d) on chessed

I suggest that he adds this sentence in to prevent anyone from reading his argument in the ways above. All human beings must share every aspect of G-d Who created the world.

The problem is that that all distinctions can become invidious; and that malicious or insensitive students may try to dismiss such clarifications as disingenuous apologetics for the censor. So if we are to legitimate such rhetoric or theology in our midst (even without agreeing with it), we need to set clear **halakhic and hashkafic** boundaries that, if breached, will demonstrate that human life is not being given infinite value.

Here are my suggestions.

1.

The status of *tzelem Elokim* must not be subject to any notion of "greater" or "lesser." All human beings are created *b'tzelem Elokim*, period.

2.

It must be a given that Jewish and non-Jewish physical lives are in practice absolutely equal infinities. For example, in a pandemic, one cannot suggest that Jews be given priority for care, or for immunization, or even that Jewish self-care responsibilities are greater because of some non-equivalence.

One of the tiny, fleeting comforts of this terrible time has been the broad acceptance within Orthodoxy that the disease is a human problem and that how to respond is a problem of human ethics. Even those whose practical decisions seem to show a willful disregard for human life at least do so without obvious prejudice. May that merit help bring us to a time of much greater comfort.

Every Jew has a right to participate in the process of Halakhic interpretation, at every level.

Chapter 8

A SEAT AT THE TABLE, AND ON THE SANHEDRIN

Every once in a while, a section of Tanakh comes and just smacks you upside the head like a flounder. How could I not have known that? Why did the opposite always seem obvious?

Converts cannot have hereditary portions in the Land of Israel. How could they, when the Land was fully distributed to the Tribes by Yehoshua?! Furthermore, Mishnah Bikkurim 1:4 rules that converts cannot read the Bikkurim declaration "because they cannot say: '(*the land) that Hashem promised to our ancestors to give to us*'". Rabbeinu Tam even suggested that converts cannot be obligated to recite the Grace after Meals because the second blessing expresses gratitude for the Land! Obviously, converts have no share in the Land.

So I was fish-smacked by Yechezkel 47:21-23:

You must divide this land to yourselves,
to the tribes of Israel.
It will be that you will make it fall-by-lot as a homestead to
yourselves,
and to the gerim/converts who are gar/dwell among you,
who have sired children in your midst.
They shall be to you
like the ezrach/citizen of the Children of Israel;
with you they will fall-by-lot into homestead,
in the midst of the Tribes of Israel.
It will be in the tribe with which the convert dwells –
there you will place his homestead.
The word of Hashem Elokim.

וְחִלַּקְתֶּם אֶת־הָאָרֶץ הַזֹּאת לָכֶם
לְשִׁבְטֵי יִשְׂרָאֵל
וְהָיָה תַּפִּלוּ אוֹתָהּ בְּנַחֲלָה
לָכֶם

וְלַהַגֵּרִים֙ הַגָּרִ֣ים בְּתוֹכְכֶ֔ם
אֲשֶׁר־הוֹלִ֥דוּ בָנִ֖ים בְּתוֹכְכֶ֑ם
וְהָי֣וּ לָכֶ֗ם
כְּאֶזְרָח֙ בִּבְנֵ֣י יִשְׂרָאֵ֔ל
אִתְּכֶם֙ יִפְּל֣וּ בְנַחֲלָ֔ה
בְּת֖וֹךְ שִׁבְטֵ֥י יִשְׂרָאֵֽל.
וְהָיָ֣ה בַשֵּׁ֔בֶט אֲשֶׁר־גָּ֥ר הַגֵּ֖ר אִתּ֑וֹ
שָׁ֚ם תִּתְּנ֣וּ נַחֲלָת֔וֹ
נְאֻ֖ם אֲדֹנָ֥י יְקֹוִֽק׃ ס

True, the halakhic consensus is that converts <u>are</u> obligated to recite the grace after meals. True, the land as a whole is given to the collective Jewish people, including the converts among us. Many also rule that converts must read the Bikkurim declaration, on the ground that the Torah etymologizes Avraham as *av hamon goyim = father of (converts from) many nations*. But if all the Land was distributed to families in the initial lottery, how can converts obtain a share? Perhaps this is one of the contradictions between Yechezkel and Torah that Chananya ben Chizkiyah stayed up all night resolving in order to keep Yechezkel off the banned books list (Chagigah 13a).

But the standard traditional commentaries don't seem bothered. See for example Metzudat David 47:22:

with you they will fall-by-lot =
they will inherit homesteads together with you.
אתכם יפלו =
עמכם יירשו בנחלה

As for the land being fully divided amongst the "original" clans – Abravanel spells out a standard resolution:

But why was this not also so in Yehoshua's division of the Land? Because the *erev rav* that ascended with Israel from Mitzrayim did not join them in their exile, and did not suffer their sufferings; rather, when they saw their success and redemption, they mixed into them, as Shemot 12:38 says: *Also an erev rav/mixed multitude ascended with them*, because they joined them only in their time of ascension, not before then, and also because they became a stumbling rock and tripping block to the Children of Israel in the Golden Calf episode and the other occasions of sin in the wilderness, and therefore it was not fitting for them to merit gaining homesteads with them.

But regarding the Future-To-Come, the prophet did not say here that the converts who would join them in the time of Redemption would homestead with the Children of Israel, because the Sages already said (Yebamot 24b) that "we must not accept converts in the Days of the Messiah"; rather he commanded this regarding the converts who dwelled among the Jews in Israel's time of exile and accepted the holy covenant and endured the suffering of exile, because it is fit for them, that just as they became Israel to endure suffering, so too they should be part of the homesteading of the land, and this is what (Yechezkel 47:21-23) means . . . that they will take their share of the good which Hashem will give-as-benefit to Israel = שמהטוב אשר יטיב השם לישראל - יקחו חלקם.

On this understanding, contemporary converts and their descendants will have full hereditary shares in the Land when it is reapportioned in Messianic times.

I read Abravanel's last line as a deliberate allusion to Bamidbar 10:33, where Mosheh promises his in-laws that if they remain with the Jews,

וְהָיָה כִּי־תֵלֵךְ עִמָּנוּ
וְהָיָה|
הַטּוֹב הַהוּא אֲשֶׁר יֵיטִיב יְקֹוָק עִמָּנוּ
וְהֵטַבְנוּ לָךְ
It will be that if you travel with us,
then it will be that
the good which Hashem will give-as-benefit to us,
we will give as benefit to you.

In other words, Mosheh promised them a share in the Land.

Torah Temimah similarly connects this verse to a beraita (Yerushalmi Bikkurim 1:4) which holds that the descendants of Yitro could recite the Bikkurim declaration in full. Kapot Temarim to Sukkah 34a explains that **all** converts can recite the declaration because it can be read as referring to the future – "*to give to us*" – and converts will have Hashem-given land in Messianic times.

Or HaChayyim takes a slightly more limited approach. He suggests that Mosheh offered Yitro a share specifically in the "Lands of Sichon and Og", i.e. TransJordan, which was not part of the original Divine promise. Or HaChayyim's approach requires Mosheh to know in advance that Sichon and Og would refuse Israel permission to cross their lands, since otherwise they would not have been conquered.

Rashi, following Sifri, points to an even more limited approach. Mosheh offered Yitro the usufruct of a vast tract around Yericho, extending all the way to Yerushalayim. Some Tannaim reported that this tract was left unapportioned in the lottery so that the Temple could be built on unapportioned land. When the Temple was built, Yitro's descendants were evicted after 440 years of tenancy.

Sifri records positions that further restrict the implications of Yechezkel 47.

> If the verses cannot relate to homesteading.
> then apply them to atonement

meaning that converts are atoned for by the sacrifices of the tribes they accompany, but have no shares in the land. Alternatively:

> If the verses cannot relate to homesteading,
> then apply them to burial

meaning that converts have a right to be buried in the Land, but not to a living share in it.

These narrower approaches recognize that Bamidbar 10:32 is Mosheh's second offer. His first offer is in 10:29

וַיֹּאמֶר מֹשֶׁה לְחֹבָב בֶּן־רְעוּאֵל הַמִּדְיָנִי חֹתֵן מֹשֶׁה
נֹסְעִים ׀ אֲנַחְנוּ אֶל־הַמָּקוֹם אֲשֶׁר אָמַר יְקֹוָק
'אֹתוֹ אֶתֵּן לָכֶם'
לְכָה אִתָּנוּ וְהֵטַבְנוּ לָךְ
כִּי־יְקֹוָק דִּבֶּר־טוֹב עַל־יִשְׂרָאֵל:

Mosheh said to Chovev ben Reuel the Midianite, Mosheh's in-law:
We are traveling to the place about which Hashem said
"I will give it to you";
go with us and we will do well by you
for Hashem spoke of doing well by Israel.

These positions read the first offer as specifically excluding any land rights:

*the place about which Hashem said "I will give it **to you**" –*
and not converts.

Yitro (or Chovev) rejects this offer in 10:30:

וַיֹּאמֶר אֵלָיו
לֹא אֵלֵךְ
:כִּי אִם־אֶל־אַרְצִי וְאֶל־מוֹלַדְתִּי אֵלֵךְ
He said to him:
I will not go
rather I will go to my land and to my culture.

Sifri records a position in which Mosheh's second offer is also rejected, presumably because it still implies second-class citizenship.

What sort of negotiation is taking place? Many commentaries understand Mosheh as interested in preserving Yitro's status as a powerful symbol of the persuasive truth of Judaism: "If you leave now, everyone will say that your conversion was for gain, and you left when the gain was disappointing." If that is correct, then perhaps Yitro's reply should be understood as: "If your religion is true, then how can you not give converts genuinely equal status? Isn't that both unjust and hypocritical, when your own Torah says *there must be one law for them, for the convert and the citizen*"?!

Chizkuni acknowledges the moral force of Yitro's argument. He understands Mosheh's first response as rooted in a claim that his hands are bound by Halakhah.

וְהֵטַבְנוּ לָךְ - מִן הַשָּׁלָל,
אֲבָל לָתֵת לוֹ חֵלֶק בָּאָרֶץ –
לֹא הָיָה הָרְשׁוּת בְּיָדָם

we will do well by you - from the spoils we take,
but to give him a portion in the land –
that authority was not in their hands.

But when Yitro rejects that offer, Mosheh finds a loophole – the verse excluding converts does not apply to lands conquered beyond G-d's original grant. Maybe that was enough to satisfy Yitro – Ramban thinks it was – but maybe not.

Keli Yakar adopts a wholly different approach.

וְאח"כ
הִבְטִיחוֹ בְּטוֹבָה רוּחָנִית
שֶׁיִּהְיֶה מִכְּלַל הַסַּנְהֶדְרִין
שֶׁנִּקְרְאוּ עֵינֵי הָעֵדָה
כמ"ש *וְהָיִיתָ לָּנוּ לְעֵינַיִם*

After (Yitro rejected the first offer)
Mosheh promised him a spiritual good
namely that he would be included in the Sanhedrin
who are called *"the eyes of the congregation"*
as 10:31 says *"and you will be eyes for us"*

Mosheh's second offer was not land but authority. He promised Yitro a seat on the Sanhedrin, a full share in making the laws. (We will leave for another time how this promise can be squared with the halakhah excluding converts from positions of *serarah*.)

If Yitro accepted this version of the second offer, then I suggest that he joined the Sanhedrin with the express ambition of modifying halakhah to give converts fully equal land-inheritance rights. Perhaps the verses in Yechezkel reflect his success. But then the Mishnah and Sifri and Rabbeinu Tam all pushed back against that outcome, and also met with some success. The moral history of halakhic interpretation is not linear.

Yitro voluntarily accepted all of halakhah as binding even while maintaining his moral critique of certain halakhot. That is a powerful lesson for our generation. But Yitro converted only after Mosheh acknowledged that all those subject to halakhah must have seats at the highest and innermost tables of halakhic conversation and decision-making. That is also a powerful lesson for our generation, and specifically for those sitting at our highest and innermost tables of halakhic conversation and decision-making.

Any serious analysis of fairness must consider resources, needs, and just desserts.

Chapter 9

THE MANNA AND ECONOMIC INEQUALITY

A confession: I always thought the Torah's account of the manna falling from heaven made sense. I never noticed the contradiction between "Everyone gets what they want (or need)" and "Everybody gets exactly the same."

זֶה הַדָּבָר אֲשֶׁר צִוָּה יְקֹוָק
לִקְטוּ מִמֶּנּוּ
אִישׁ לְפִי אָכְלוֹ
עֹמֶר לַגֻּלְגֹּלֶת מִסְפַּר נַפְשֹׁתֵיכֶם
אִישׁ לַאֲשֶׁר בְּאָהֳלוֹ תִּקָּחוּ:

This is what Hashem commended:
Glean of it,
each man in accordance with his okhel
an omer *per head, in accordance with the number of your souls*
each man shall take for those who are in his tent.

One can resolve this contradiction at the price of redundancy by understanding "each man in accordance with his *okhel*" as referring to "each man shall take for those who are in his tent", so that everyone gets the same. But this reading is hard to sustain in the next sentences:

וַיַּעֲשׂוּ־כֵן בְּנֵי יִשְׂרָאֵל
וַיִּלְקְטוּ
הַמַּרְבֶּה וְהַמַּמְעִיט:
וַיָּמֹדּוּ בָעֹמֶר
וְלֹא הֶעְדִּיף הַמַּרְבֶּה וְהַמַּמְעִיט לֹא הֶחְסִיר
אִישׁ לְפִי־אָכְלוֹ לָקָטוּ.

Bnei Yisroel did so.
They gleaned,
the increaser and the diminisher.
They measured as/via an omer.
The increaser did not get extra
and the diminisher did not lose out.

Each man in accordance with his okhel *they gleaned.*

Who are the "increaser" and "diminisher?" To be consistent, we must claim that they are men with larger and smaller households. They must measure an *omer* per person, not an overall *omer*. But then why would we expect the increaser to get extra, and the diminisher to lose out? And overall, why is it necessary for the Torah to explain at such length the simple idea that the manna was collected and/or distributed proportionally?

Leaving aside the literary issues: Why would it be good and proper for everyone to receive the same, rather than in accordance with their needs or wants?

Ibn Ezra and Avraham ben HaRambam stake out diametrically opposite positions.

According to Ibn Ezra, an *omer* per head was the maximum, but children got less. He does not explain whether **adults** received the same regardless of the size of their body or appetite, and his reading fits very poorly with "The increaser did not get extra and the diminisher did not lose out." (Chatam Sofer reaches Ibn Ezra's outcome by arguing that the term "*omer*" should be understood as a subjective volume measurement, based on each person's fingerwidth. This requires an assumption that fingerwidth directly correlated with bodysize.)

According to Avraham ben HaRambam, "This is one of the wonders of the manna and its wondrous signs, that it fed equally the adult and the minor, the strong and the weak, each one needing exactly an *omer* per head."

Avraham ben HaRambam's position seems to me much better literarily than Ibn Ezra's. The Torah's repetitions and paradoxes are intended to emphasize that the manna miraculously squared the circle by making an equal share satisfy everyone's needs equally.

But I'm not sure what this reading *means*, what its message is. In real life, individual needs and desires differ. Avraham ben HaRambam seems to think that the message is that we don't really need more than just enough. (Ralbag adds that we shouldn't think it virtuous to get by with less than enough. The manna critiques both hedonists and ascetics.) This philosophy provides a demand-centric approach to inequality – let's train everyone to recognize their true needs, because true needs are much less unequal than desires.

One can accept this reading but challenge the moral. Even if we all boil our needs down to be conceptually alike, some people's basic needs will consume vastly more resources than others', e.g., if they have certain medical conditions. The manna miraculously matched equality of income with equality of outcome, but what should we do in our world, where they don't match?

So far we've only dealt with two axes – resources/wealth and needs/desires. But any serious treatment of fairness has to consider a third axis: just desserts. Is it obvious that all people deserve the same share of resources, or to have their needs/desires equally met? Even if we assume the propriety of "from each according to their abilities," perhaps the proper formula is "To each a share of their needs proportional to the share of their abilities that they contribute."

Rabbi Samson Raphael Hirsch may accept a version of this formula:

> "However, it seems that the intent of the gleaners to glean, each in accordance with his quota, was an unalterable condition, because otherwise they would have been able to suffice – once the outcome of the first day became known to them – with collecting a minimal amount, as one way or the other, each person would receive sufficient for their needs, and no one would under any circumstances receive more than their quota."

One wonders, however, at the psychological impact of this arrangement. This is make-work in the purest sense. In yeshivish terms, it strips away the illusion that human effort/*hishtadlut* has any direct relevance to results.

Mekhilta d'Rabbi Shimon bar Yochai may provide a slightly different approach.

איש לפי אכלו –
דורשי רשומות אומרים:

מיכן שהיה בו במן
בזעת אפך תאכל לחם
each man in accordance with his okhel –
The expounders of reshumot say:
From here we learn that the manna contained within itself
by the sweat of your brow shall you eat bread

This may mean that G-d had a principled objection to providing human beings with food that required no effort on their part. If so, maybe a token, minimal effort was sufficient after the first day.

This suggests that G-d used the manna to create an egalitarian utopia. All needs were provided for equally, and with minimal effort. Having one's needs provided for was a human right, not something one needed to earn, and there was nothing one person could do to become more deserving than another of having his or her needs met. In our world, we should strive as best we can to recreate such equality.

What if someone wanted more?

We all know that the manna was an every-flavor bean. What if some people had much greater gustatory imaginations than others, and so they experienced the manna more pleasurably than others?

Ramban plays the Faucian skunk at the egalitarian picnic. He notes that *benei Yisroel* ask to return to Egypt where they "*sat over the fleshpot, and ate bread to satiety*," and G-d responded with quail and manna – but there is no miraculous equalization with regard to quail.

ויתכן שהיו גדוליהם לוקטין אותו,
או שהיה מזדמן לחסידים שבהם,
וצעיריהם היו תאבים לו ורעבים ממנו,
כי לא יספר בשלו
וילקטו המרבה והממעיט
כאשר אמר במן.
Plausibly the adult/great/powerful? among them would glean the quail,
or the quail would present themselves only to the pious among them,
and the youngsters would desire it and be hungry for lack of it,
because the Torah does not tell regarding the quail
"they gleaned, the increaser and the diminisher"

as it said regarding the manna.

Human beings do not live by bread alone, and the manna did not succeed in creating a society with no desires beyond its needs, if that was its intent. G-d did not create a fully equal society – if Ramban's second hypothesis is correct, He seems to have deliberately generated material inequality based on spiritual inequality.

Perhaps G-d deliberately created human beings as too complex for any notion of sameness to yield fairness. The manna teaches that sameness must nonetheless be part of the equation.

PART III

HALAKHIC METHODS

"Rules of authority" decisors may be oxymoronic in the sense that they are unwilling to make decisions.

Chapter 10

THE TRUTH OF THE PROCESS?
TECHNOHALAKHAH and TECHUMIN

There are two kinds of halakhic decisors.

Some like to make decisions based on rules of authority or procedure. There are lots of such rules, e.g. "The halakhah does not follow the position of a student when in dispute with their teacher"; "When Rabbi Akiva disputes with a peer, the halakhah follows Rabbi Akiva"; "The law follows the later authority (within the same era)"; and the classic "When a doubt arises regarding a Biblical law, follow the stringent position; when a doubt arises regarding a Rabbinic law, follow the lenient position". (See the article הלכה in the Encyclopedia Talmudit.)

Other like to make decision based on the merits of the issue.

This second category can be subdivided. "Merit" can mean the position that best fits the language of Tannaitic and Amoraic sources; or that best fits what one sees as the mainstream interpretation of those sources; or that best fulfills what one understands as the purpose of the law; or that best coheres conceptually; or that best coheres intuitively.

All the above relates to the abstract question "What is the law?" rather than to the concrete question "What is the law in this case?". There are also two sorts of cases: those in which all the human interests are on one side, and those in which two or more parties have opposed interests.

Decisors may be radically different as case-judges than as law-judges. Those who use rules of authority to decide law may be focused entirely on the needs of justice or piety or health in deciding specific cases; those who focus on merits when deciding the law may decide cases mechanically on the basis of the law as it has been determined, without considering the impact of their decisions on the specific people involved.

"Merit" decisors must acknowledge the existence of rules of authority. But they correctly point out that such rules are mostly presented as defaults in case of doubt, not as overriding principles. When one is certain that the lenient side of a dispute about Biblical law is correct, one may follow it; when one is certain that the stringent side of a dispute about Rabbinic law is correct, one must not follow it.

So "rules of authority" decisors may be oxymoronic in the sense that they are unwilling to make decisions, or alternatively, may be unable to tolerate the uncertainty inherent in any substantive decision.

Unwillingness to make decisions can spread to the rules of authority. Is this a case of a student arguing with a teacher, or of a later authority arguing with an earlier? What if Rabbi Akiva's position is disputed by a later Tanna? This leads to a third kind of decisor, the one who seeks to satisfy all positions. This third kind of decisor can also emerge out of those focused on substance, if they give themselves over entirely to understanding their predecessors' positions rather than to evaluating them.

Rhetoric and method must be carefully distinguished. For some poskim, the mechanical rules somehow end up disproportionately favoring the positions they see as "meritorious".

Actual decisors, like actual human beings, are generally hybrids rather than ideal types. For example, a decisor may be rule-based generally but merit-based in a few specialties where they have greater substantive confidence, or merit-based except for areas where they find the overall contours of the law unintelligible (chukim). Also, even decisors with generally strong and self-aware methodological commitments may override them roughshod when dealing with issues that activate them ideologically.

All the above is intended as pure description, and to a certain extent as autodescription. Let's move now to a brief and sketchy forward-looking conversation about the way a particular rule-of-authority might interact with substantive concerns in a specific area of halakhah.

Halakhic practices can be revived, or go dormant, as the result of personalities or technology. For example, the revival of shatnez checking in America is often attributed to the indefatigable Mr. Joseph

Rosenberger, who came up with both new methods of testing and catchy ad campaigns. (My favorite was the person, first zapped by lightning and then turned away at Gan Eden, moaning: "But the salesman told me it had no linen in it!") I've explained in episode three of the ongoing Efshar Leverurei podcast series that it's not at all clear how necessary shatnez testing is for which garments as a matter of pure halakhah, or perhaps more sharply, that Mr. Rosenberger made it much more necessary halakhically by making it much more easily accessible. By the same token, the ritual of "checking ingredients" before purchasing food was largely obsolesced by the advent of industrial kashrut organizations. (It is encouraging and educationally necessary to publicize the occasional comic bloopers like certified ham, lest the next generation grow up to believe that certification **makes** food kosher. Indeed, in the bad old days, fraudulent rabbis would offer to "bless" products for manufacturers.)

My sense is that the issue of *techumin* on Shabbat (very roughly the prohibition against travelling more than 2000 *amot* in any direction from one's point of origin) was largely out of public consciousness in America until thirty years ago. Part of this may have been the result of ignorance. But my suspicion is that *talmidei chakhamim* and *amei haaretz* alike shared an intuition that *techumin* were not intended to forbid walks that were perceived of as staying within one's urban space, which halakhically is considered to be "4 amot" no matter how large it gets, rather than travelling to a different space. The issue is that the halakhic definition of "urban space" does not match our intuition. For example, halakhah appears to define any space where houses are more than approximately 235 feet apart (depending on the size one chooses for an *amah*) as distinct. But there are many "cities' which contain spaces where such distances are common.

The conventional explanation for this discrepancy is that the Talmudic city was the highly concentrated center of an agricultural settlement, with the farmers clustering together and walking out to their fields in various directions. This seems a plausible but insufficient explanation for why the issue has become stark now rather than much earlier in the post-Talmudic era. I would instead point to two other factors. The first is the development of "urban sprawl" in the age of the automobile. This really should have created a crisis, but a combination of suburban halakhic indifference and intuition let us ignore the issue. Then GPS technology and Google Earth made the gap between apparent law and reality too obvious to ignore. Technohalakhists who've never left their own *daled amot* can produce maps for anywhere in the world – your suburban estate, your bungalow colony, etc. – that show exactly how far apart houses are in your area, and therefore draw your halakhic Shabbat-walk border with absolute clarity.

Except this clarity is often an illusion. Halakhah contains an array of devices for expanding the *techum*. Some of these are consensus, but many, many questions seem to have first arisen recently, and I suspect that more attempts at comprehensive restatements of the law have been written in the past three decades than in the previous three millennia.

To give one example. I said above "2000 amot in any direction from one's point of origin" – actually it is the square within which one can inscribe a circle with a radius of 2000 amot centered on one's point of origin. One gets more than 2000 amot 'in the corners' of the square. This is simple enough when one's point of origin is indeed a point (or even "the square within which one can inscribe a circle with a radius of 4 amot from one's ur-point of origin"). But halakhah expands the point of origin to include the entire urban area surrounding it. More – for many cities, halakhah expands the point of origin to include the North-South oriented square circumscribed around the city using the furthest point on each directional axis as the basis for its line. (Then to find the *techum*, one extends that square 2000 amot in every direction, and then squares off the result. I'm leaving out steps, and possibly making mistakes – please do not use this as a guide for practice.)

It should be clear that one city's square may include part or all of what initially seemed to be a wholly separate city, or that two cities' squares can intersect. The question then is whether the intersection of squares unifies them halakhically (and whether one then squares the resulting unit before extending the 2000 amot.) If intersecting squares are enough to create a unitary "point of origin", many of the clashes between intuition and law can be evaded. On the other hand, clashes may develop in the opposite direction, where e.g. intuition rebels against the notion that the entire Eastern Seaboard is one point for *techum* purposes.

Talmud Eiruvin 46a records a rule of authority that "the law follows the lenient authority regarding issues of eiruv". Let's assume (I think very defensibly) that this includes all matters of *techum*, and not just those associated with the institution of *eiruv techumin*; and that it applies to post-Talmudic disputes as well; and that it applies even to newly-raised issues where many outcomes are plausible.

What I tentatively suggest is that decisors can and should see this rule not as a mandate to mechanically adopt the "lenient" position in every dispute, but rather as license to construct a coherent body of law that makes intuitive sense to their constituents.

If you need a verse to tell you that you can't kill someone else to save your own life, then you can't interpret Torah properly at all. Your errors will cascade. But if there's no space for Torah to challenge even deeply held convictions, what is the point of learning?

Chapter 11

WHEN TORAH CLASHES WITH OUR VALUES

We all censor Torah. We all have rigid rules about what Torah cannot mean, and tools to make sure it means something else.

Censorship is mostly about protecting ourselves from the text. Readers who genuinely feel bound by a text try to prevent it from teaching things they disagree with: *Rabbi, how can the Torah be critiquing Orthodox society?* Readers at risk of feeling bound by a text try to prevent it from teaching things they agree with, especially with regard to issues on which they've staked their autonomy: *If the prohibition against pork isn't an obsolete health regulation, do we have to keep kosher?*

This is ok. We should come to Torah with rigid assumptions, especially moral principles (*sevarot*). If you need a Biblical verse to tell you that you can't kill someone else to save your own life, i.e. if you don't know without being told that "*what makes your blood redder than his?*" is a rhetorical question, then you can't interpret Torah properly at all. Your errors will cascade.

But one should not come to Torah with very many such assumptions. Torah must be able to challenge even deeply held convictions, or else what is the point of learning?

The areas of sex, gender, sexuality, and politics are especially fraught for Torah interpreters nowadays, because audiences who feel bound by Torah are more likely to censor than to consider ideas they disagree with, and the censoring is likely to be forceful. I presume this is true of myself as a reader. And yet, I think it is vital that we maintain the capacity to learn from Torah on these issues. I also recognize that almost everyone in these conversations feels deeply threatened by interpretations they disagree with.

So I want to try something. This essay is a collection of raw, first-level interpretive observations – they provide ways of thinking through the Torah narrative without (I think) imposing any conclusions, so that defenses can be deployed after learning rather than before. You're welcome to send me your thoughts about what these interpretations could mean for these issues, or to politely post them (and equally politely critique such posts), and of course to challenge or support them at the level of the text.

1.

In the first Creation narrative, the human male and female <u>work</u> together, facing the world, but have no need to <u>be</u> together and face each other. They communicate pragmatic instructions but not interiority. That's how it must be, because experience is incommunicable across difference.

In the second Creation narrative, G-d serves as the miraculous common ground that enables communication across difference. Intimacy between male and female therefore requires G-d to be present in the relationship.

The above is Rav Joseph B. Soloveitchik's reading in "The Lonely Man of Faith". But that essay has an astonishing gap. That male and female are different is a vital element of the thesis. But the Rav never tells us anything about **how** male and female differ. Reversing the sex (and gender) of the characters would change nothing about his analysis.

But we can try to color in the Rav's portraiture within the lines he drew.

Adam Two is lonely, and then discovers companionship. Eve Two is never lonely that we know of.

Adam Two is aware of the difference between being alone and being lonely, because he has experienced unsatisfying companionship. Eve marries the first being she meets.

Is this why Eve is vulnerable to seduction by the snake – because she suddenly realizes that Adam is not everything one could wish for in a husband, and she has no reason to settle for less than perfection?

Does Adam eat the fruit after Eve because he'd rather die than be alone again, and he does not believe that Eve is replaceable (=she is his *bashert*)? Does Eve eat the fruit because having never experienced loneliness, she has no fear of death?

2.

In the first Creation narrative, humanity is commanded to be fruitful and multiply, but no children are born. So far as we know, every other created thing fulfills the promises and destinies that G-d assigns them (although sometimes with persnickety variations). But human beings do not. (Deborah Klapper claims that the same is true of everything else as well – no children are born to any species, etc.) Is this part of why Rashi understands the first narrative as a hypothetical, as what would have happened had G-d created the world via pure justice, whereas the second narrative is a metaphor for the world as we know it?

3.

> *Hashem Elokim took the adam*
> *He placed him the arbor of Eden*
> *to cultivate and protect it.*
> *Hashem Elokim imposed a commandment on the adam, saying:*
> *"From all the trees of the arbor –*
> *you may/must certainly eat.*
> *but from the tree of knowledge of good and bad –*
> *you must not eat from it*
> *because on the day you eat from it –*
> *you may/must certainly die."*
> *Hashem Elokim said:*
> *It is not good, the adam being alone*
> *I will make for him a support parallel to him = ezer k'negdo.*
> *Hashem Elokim formed from the earth/adamah*
> *all the chayot of the field, and all the fliers of the heavens,*
> *He brought (?each?) to the adam to see what he would name it*
> [or: He brought each to the adam to see what would call to him)
> *Everything that the adam called a nefesh chayah –*
> *that was its name.*

The adam called names
to all the cattle and to all the fliers of the heavens
and to the chayah of the field
but for the adam
he did not find a support parallel to him.

Immediately after commanding the *adam* to avoid knowledge of *tov* and *ra*, Hashem Elokim states that "it is not-*tov*, the *adam* being alone". This means that the *adam* would violate the command by becoming aware that he is lonely (unless one understands the command as forbidding only a specific means of obtaining the knowledge). Yet Hashem Elokim immediately sets out to make him aware of just that. Why?

4.

How does the *adam* become aware of his loneliness? He tries and fails to bond with other creatures from the *adamah*. The *adam* even goes on non-*shiddukh* dates with the cattle, i.e. with domesticated animals, even though Hashem Elokim never brought them to him.

Rashi famously cites the midrashic reading in which the *adam*'s dates are actually assignations. This might mean that the *adam* was capable of finding emotionally sufficient nonsexual companionship with other species (dogs? dolphins?), but that he could not connect emotion to *eros*, and only the combination could relieve his loneliness.

Or it might mean that the *adam* harbored the hope and belief that *eros* was sufficient regardless of the nonsexual relationship.

Is it obvious that G-d brings only the female of each species to the *adam*? If so, does the *adam* know that they have male mates of their own species, or does G-d take the Randian position that rational males can be expected to politely give way to a male who is a superior match for the female in question (because there can be no conflict of interest among rational persons)?

My underlying question is whether Hashem Elokim is leading the *adam* to discover his sexual orientation, as distinct from his sexual attraction. Moreover, does the *adam* know that he is expected to find an *ezer k'negdo*, or might he think that Hashem Elokim is genuinely interested in his Linnaean analysis of the animal kingdom? Why is it not valuable for the *ishah* to engage in a similar exploration before being giftwrapped and presented to the *adam*? (Deborah Klapper sees no reason for the experiences of "first human" and "second human" to be mapped essentially onto "male" and "female").

5.

Conservative: Human beings were created last because everything in the nonconscious world was created for the sake of human beings . .
.

Liberal: Human beings were created last because their purpose is to care for the nonconscious world . . .

Conservative: . . . and therefore women are the apex of creation.

Liberal: . . . and therefore women are responsible to care for men.

Narrator: Are you sure that your positions haven't gotten muddled?

6.

Conservative: G-d gave us a perfect world. We ruined it by imposing our own independent notions of good and bad, and got cursed for our pains. That should teach us to leave well enough alone.

Liberal: So we should just leave it ruined?

7.

Is it important for students to be taught that they can wreck the world as much as repair it? Does this question have a specifically Jewish answer? I posted these questions on Facebook and received a variety of serious responses to the first question, but nobody contended that Jews and Judaism had something special to say about the issue. This conflicted with my sense that *tikkun olam* is often taught *davka* to override this lesson, and as uniquely Jewish. So I'll reframe the challenge more directly: What traditional Jewish sources, if any, have the theme or moral that one should be temperamentally cautious about bold moral movements because of the risk of unintended consequences?

Rav Chaim Vital's claim that the halakhah of Messianic times will follow Beit Shammai flatters us by suggesting that our spiritual instincts are too good for this unredeemed world.

Chapter 12

LEARNING TORAH WE DISAGREE WITH

In the realm of halakhah, Modern Orthodoxy celebrates theoretical pluralism. Beit Shammai are halakhically irrelevant (*eyno mishnah*) when they disagree with Beit Hillel, and yet are *divrei Elokim chayyim* and therefore (equally?) worthy of our time and effort interpreting them.

However, public shiurim rarely focus on rejected halakhic positions. Even Beit Shammai's position is most often used as a foil to develop Beit Hillel's position by contrast. It is a safe foil, because everyone knows which way the halakhah must end up, even if they find Beit Shammai's position more compelling.

Discussing Beit Shammai trains us to live comfortably with a certain amount of religious dissonance. If we accept Rav Chaim Vital's claim that the halakhah of Messianic times will follow Beit Shammai, the experience may even be flattering and affirming; our spiritual instincts are too good for this unredeemed world.

Beit Shammai's position is also safer than most because its rejection (according to the more popularly known Talmudic position) results from a Heavenly voice rather than from human reason, and because the Talmud explains Beit Hillel's triumph as a result of character. Indeed, because Beit Hillel's superiority is embodied in their willingness to cite Beit Shammai's position before their own, our willingness to explicate Beit Shammai's positions actually cements our identification with Beit Hillel.

So it makes sense that few public shiurim are devoted to making sense of non-Beit Shammai halakhic positions that the teacher thinks shouldn't be followed. I suspect that the more tenuous the authority of the approved position, the less generosity shown the rejected positions.

What about the realm of *hashkofoh*? Do we see value in expounding the theological, moral, or ethical positions found in the Tradition that, in our opinion, should be rejected?

There are at least two ways to reject the premise of this question. One way is to deny that binding decisions exist in the realm of *hashkofoh*. The other is to deny that important disagreements exist[3].

But let's suppose that the Tradition in fact contains hashkafic positions that should be rejected as guides for practice. Is there value in expounding those positions in and of themselves?[4] Or is that irresponsible?

This question often comes up for me in the process of preparing a parashat hashavua essay or shiur. I generally start by reading through the parshah until I find a section that raises new questions for me, or old but disturbingly unresolved questions. Then I go through the commentaries on Al HaTorah and/or Bar Ilan, sometimes with supplements from paper books, until I find one that makes me rethink. But making me rethink doesn't mean that I'll end up agreeing with it. I might end up strongly disagreeing. Can I still base my essay or shiur on it? Can divrei Torah end with morals we disagree with? Or even that we're not sure whether we agree with?

The rest of this essay focuses on a Ramban that met the requirement above – it made me rethink – but I'm not sure yet how I'll feel about it when I'm done. I'm writing stream-of-consciousness to model the idea that there is value in thinking about challenging interpretations of Torah, and in sharing our understandings of such Torah, even if we won't necessarily agree, or at least not agree fully, with the hashkafic perspectives that emerge from them.

---

[3] (The first position is articulated at least with regard to ethics by Rav Yosef Dov Soloveitchik in <u>Halakhic Morality</u>, and the second by Rav Eliyahu Dessler in <u>Michtav MeiEliyahu.</u> Each of them acknowledges that many *hashkafic* positions are utterly incompatible with Torah; the discussion is only with regard to positions that have already made it into the Tradition.)

[4] (Full disclosure: I often teach Rav Dessler's position as a foil.)

Ramban to Shemot 1:10 wonders why Pharaoh's campaign against the Jews was launched gradually and subtly rather than with sudden overwhelming force. He offers three reasons in the context of an overall vision of the narrative arc:

> Pharaoh and the experts who advised him did not see fit to smite them with the sword, because
> 1) this would be a great betrayal, to smite without cause the nation that had entered the land at the command of a prior king
> 2) also, the populace would not have permitted the king to do such criminal violence, and he is consulting with them
> 3) Furthermore, the Jews themselves were a numerous and strong people, and would have made full-scale war against him
> Instead, Pharaoh said *hava nitchakmah lo* – let us be clever so that the Jews will not realize that they are being treated with hatred. So he imposed a labor levy on them, which was standard practice for communities of resident aliens, as we can see from Shlomoh's practice in 1Kings 9:21. Then he covertly commanded the midwives to kill the male infants at birth, so that even the birthing mothers would not realize what they were doing. Then he ordered his entire people "every male that is born – you shall throw them into the Nile", meaning: He did not wish to order his executioners to kill them with the king's sword, or to have the executioners be the ones throwing them into the Nile, but rather said to his people: When anyone among you finds a male Jewish infant, throw him into the Nile, and if the father comes to the king or to the local official, they will tell him: Bring witnesses and vengeance will be done to the perpetrator!. Once the king's 'whip was untied', the Mitzriyim would search the Jewish houses, enter them at night ?as if they were strangers? and remove the children from them, which is what the Torah refers to

by saying "And (Yocheved) was no longer able to hide (Mosheh)".

It seems that this situation was only briefly in force, as there was no such decree when Aharon was born, and after Mosheh's birth it seems to have lapsed. Perhaps Pharaoh's daughter out of her pity for Mosheh told her father not to behave so, or perhaps once it became known that the decree came from the king it lapsed, or perhaps it the decree was made specifically then on the basis of astrology, as per our masters (Shemot Rabbah 1:29). All this was done with cleverness toward them so that the criminality would remain unknown. This is the meaning of their saying to Mosheh our Teacher (Shemot 5:21) "You have given us a bad odor so as to give a sword into their hand", because now they will hate us more, and they will find grounds for accusing us of revolt and killing us openly in front of everyone rather than resorting to trickery.

Reason #3 is pragmatic – Pharaoh chose the gradual approach in the belief that it would prevent the Jews from taking up arms to protect themselves. This may have been good policy – it seems to have worked – although I can imagine situations in which the element of surprise is more valuable.

Reason #2 makes a claim about a rift between the ruling elite and the populace. Ramban does not explain why the populace would be less inclined to genocide against the Jews than the elite. Perhaps they had lingering gratitude for Yoseph's policies; or perhaps in general he believes that the common sense of the masses is less prone to immoral extremes than that of the elite. Or – and I think this most likely – genocidal extremism is generally rare, so whichever group gets to that point first has to worry that the other won't go along.

Reason #1 interests me most. Ramban's language suggests that this was an internal constraint on Pharaoh, that he simply could not bring himself to commit so sudden a betrayal. The gradualism was necessary to overcome his own *yetzer hatov*. I'm not sure, however, that the best reading of the story indicates any psycho-moral development within the original enslaving Pharaoh.

Rabbeinu Bachya understood Ramban differently. He inserts the phrase

ותהיה זאת למלך לחרפה בתוך העמים
because this would be a disgrace for the king among the nations

This suggests yet a different external constraint. But I wonder to what extent he is correct that political leaders within one group are constrained by the moral disregard of leaders in another group, at least once they've reached an internal state consistent with the commission of genocide. I also wonder again whether gradualism is a better tactic than surprise for avoiding international condemnation – that doesn't seem to be the lesson of Rwanda or Bosnia.

Finally, Ramban suggests that the directly genocidal technique of throwing babies in the river was short-lived, and offers as one possible explanation for its short-livedness that Pharaoh was persuaded by his daughter to stop.

Overall, the message of Ramban seems to be that there were many people who could have prevented the enslavement of the Jews and killing of our sons. His daughter might have spoken up earlier; the populace might have maintained their moral revulsion; or the international community might have condemned him. At each stage, their opposition might have had not only a pragmatic but a moral impact. Perhaps this Pharaoh was incapable of hardening his heart?

But Pharaoh's most subtle technique was at the second stage. He encouraged the Egyptians to victimize the Jews by promising them that the justice system would look the other way, while insisting to the Jews that they rely on the law to protect them. The Jews would not realize in time that the promise of justice was a mockery. Meanwhile, with the מורא של מלכות = the fear of government gone, the Mitzriyim may have gone further than even Pharaoh intended.

What do you think is the lesson of Ramban's understanding of the process by which we were enslaved in Egypt? Would you "give this vort over" even if you disagreed with the lesson?

The 'leprous house' is an allegory for G-d's awareness that He will eventually destroy His own house. But the allegory is against halakhah, which rules that the Temple cannot become a 'leprous house'.

Chapter 13

PURELY THEORETICAL HALAKHAH

Many rabbinic texts cannot be categorized neatly as either "Halakhah" and "Aggada". Some are hybrids, such as legal analyses that treat fantastical narratives as formal legal precedents, or narratives whose plot revolves around a legal claim or dispute. Others live near the border, incorporating superficial characteristics of the other basic type without changing their essential nature, or deliberately establishing and then flouting expectations.

None of this means that the underlying binary is useless. Deliberately flouting expectations works artistically only because there are expectations. Creativity in the absence of tradition is meaningless meandering maunder, as T.S. Eliot argued.

"Purely hypothetical law" seems likely to be a marginal type. Superficially it looks just like ordinary halakhah; the Torah discusses the law of the *bayit hamenuga* ('leprous' house) in the same apparent tone and texture as the leprous person and the leprous garment. The Sifra extracts legal detail from the relevant Torah text (Vayikra 14:33-57) in a manner that seems fully compatible with its analysis of the texts relating to the other forms of *tzora'at*. Tractate Negaim devotes two chapters that seem pretty typical of Mishnah to the *bayit hamenuga*. So when a beraita on Sanhedrin 71a (also found in Tosefta Negaim 6:1) declares that "the law of the *bayit hamenuga* never was and never will be, and why was it written? Expound and receive reward", it certainly flouts expectations. Should we classify the standard-form legal analysis of a purely hypothetical law as *aggada*?

Let's put this discussion in a context where the boundary between halakhah and aggada seems clear. Vayikra 14:34-35 reads

:

כִּי תָבֹאוּ אֶל־אֶרֶץ כְּנַעַן
אֲשֶׁר אֲנִי נֹתֵן לָכֶם לַאֲחֻזָּה
וְנָתַתִּי נֶגַע צָרַעַת
בְּבֵית אֶרֶץ אֲחֻזַּתְכֶם:
וּבָא אֲשֶׁר־לוֹ הַבַּיִת
וְהִגִּיד לַכֹּהֵן לֵאמֹר:
"כְּנֶגַע נִרְאָה לִי בַּבָּיִת":

When you arrive in Canaan,
which I am giving you as a homestead
I will place a tzora'at plague
in the house of the land of your homestead.
The one to whom the house belongs will come,
and say to the priest as follows:
"Something like a plague-stain has appeared to me in the house".

Several elements of this verse seem anomalous. "House" is singular – one would expect 'houses'. One would also expect "house in the land" rather than "of" the land, which seems to identify the house with the land. Finally, why is "homestead" repeated?

Vayikra Rabbah 17:7 provides a beautiful and comprehensive answer.

בבית ארץ אחוזתכם –
זה בהמ"ק . . .
ובא אשר לו הבית –
זה הקדוש ברוך הוא

In the house of the land of your homestead –
this refers to the Holy Temple . . .
The one to whom the house belongs will come –
this refers to the Holy Blessed One . . .

The *bayit hamenuga* is an allegory for G-d's awareness that He will eventually feel compelled to destroy His own house, when it is irretrievably defiled by idolatry. The destruction of the Temple is also a metonymy for exile =the loss of the Jewish homestead.

Talmud Yoma 11b – 12a offers a very different approach.

. . . וְהָתַנְיָא:

יָכוֹל יִהְיוּ בָתֵּי כְנֵסִיּוֹת וּבָתֵּי מִדְרָשׁוֹת מְטַמְּאִין בִּנְגָעִים?

תַּלְמוּד לוֹמַר:

וּבָא אֲשֶׁר לוֹ הַבַּיִת —

מִי שֶׁמְיוּחָד לוֹ,

יָצְאוּ אֵלּוּ שֶׁאֵין מְיוּחָדִין לוֹ.

. . . והתניא:

אחזתכם —

אחזתכם מטמאה בנגעים,

ואין ירושלים מטמאה בנגעים.

אמר רבי יהודה:

אני לא שמעתי אלא מקום מקדש בלבד.

. . . הא בתי כנסיות ובתי מדרשות - מטמאין בנגעים

אימא:

'אמר רבי יהודה: אני לא שמעתי אלא מקום מקודש בלבד.'

במאי קא מיפלגי?

תנא קמא סבר: ירושלים לא נתחלקה לשבטים;

. . . ורבי יהודה סבר: ירושלים נתחלקה לשבטים

. . . But we learned in a beraita:

It would have been possible that synagogues and study halls were

subject to house-*tzora'at* –

so Scripture teaches:

The one to whom the house belongs will come –

meaning one that is reserved to someone,

excluding these that are not reserved to someone.

. . . But we learned in a beraita:

of your homestead –

your homestead is subject to house-*tzora'at*,

but Jerusalem is not subject to house-*tzora'at*.

Said Rabbi Yehudah:

I only heard that this about the place of the Holy Temple.

Bu synagogues and study halls are subject to house-*tzora'at*!?

Emend Rabbi Yehuda's statement to read:

'Said Rabbi Yehuda: I only heard this about <u>sanctified places</u>.'

What is the basis of their disagreement?

The initial position in the beraita held that

Jerusalem was not apportioned (as a homestead) among the tribes;

Rabbi Yehudah held that

Jerusalem was apportioned among the tribes.

The upshot is that according to all legal positions, the Holy Temple is not subject to house-tzora'at, whether because it was never assigned as a homestead to any tribe, or because house-tzora'at does not apply to buildings dedicated to Divine purposes. Talmud Yoma is thus diametrically opposed to the allegory in Vayikra Rabbah. The one building we can be absolutely certain cannot become a *bayit hamenuga* is the Temple.

We might suggest that Talmud Yoma is engaged in *halakhah*, whereas Vayikra Rabbah is engaged in *aggada*. A common technique of *aggada* is what I call "willing suspension of halakhic disbelief"- one is allowed to create a literary world in which one halakhah doesn't exist in order to make a narrative work. This would resolve the contradiction. But this technique may be legitimate only when it plays off established *halakhah*. Is Talmud Yoma really engaged in *halakhah* if the *bayit hamenuga* is already a legal fantasy?

Here we must note that the position that the *bayit hamenuga* "never happened and never will" is challenged in both the Tosefta and the Talmud by eyewitness reports of locations marked as the remains of such houses. Perhaps Vayikra Rabbah assumes that the *bayit* hamenuga has been and will be. Or perhaps those who regard the entire category as hypothetical see themselves as even freer to offer allegories that contradict the law. Or more radically, they see the category as beyond the reach of law.

The problem with this last proposal is that Talmud Sanhedrin identifies the "never was and never will be" camp with the most restrictive position in a halakhic dispute about the physical appearance of the plague-stain. The Tosefta may not agree with this connection, and neither Sifri nor the Mishnah mention the possibility that the *bayit hamenuga* is purely hypothetical. But Talmud Sanhedrin seems to view the author of this position as engaged in the same kind of legal analysis and taking the same kind of legal positions as his interlocutors. In other words, the Talmud indicates that the authors of this position saw themselves as engaged in the intellectual discipline of *halakhah*. Other Talmudic discussions also use legal positions taken with regard to *bayit hamenuga* as precedents for discussions of legal areas. For example, houses that are excluded from *bayit hamenuga* are presumptively also excluded from the obligation of placing a *mezuzah*.

I will venture to say, in the hope that someone will prove me wrong, that there is nothing whatsoever that makes discussions of the *bayit hamenuga* distinctive within Torah, in either form or content, other than the claim that "it never was and never will be".

Until I am proven wrong, I see two basic options.

One is to say that the hypotheticality position is a Masoretic epiphenomenon, an interesting footnote to halakhic history mentioned and considered only once in the Babylonian Talmud (and not at all in the Yerushalmi) and then largely ignored until the publication of Rabbi Joseph B. Soloveitchik's Ish HaHalakhah.

The other is to say, along with the eponym of Ish HaHalakhah, that the intellectual discipline of halakhah is not essentially related to halakhic practice. A separate pragmatic discipline of *psak* covers that. This position argues that we should not expect the fact that the law is purely hypothetical to have any practical effect on the way we study it.

The motto of the Center for Modern Torah Leadership is "Taking Responsibility for Torah". It was formulated to oppose the claim that halakhah can be discussed in the beit midrash without considering its real-world consequences. Those consequences exist, so what justifies us in ignoring them? So if there are only two options, I would have to choose the first.

There might however be hybrid options. For example, we might say that because some *poskim* use the *bayit hamenuga* as legal precedent in other areas, even those who hold that it is purely hypothetical have an ethical responsibility to consider the practical consequences of their positions. Halakhic scholars must always consider not only the utopian world where everyone accepts their *psak*, but also what will happen if not everyone *paskens* like them, for example if their correct ruling that a woman is no longer married nonetheless leads a significant part of the community to treat her subsequent children as *mamzerim*.

This hybrid changes nothing directly in practice. But maybe there is a general value and significant overall effect in recognizing that even the most practically necessary binaries are not full descriptions of reality, and conversely, that sometimes it is practically necessary to reduce exquisitely nuanced realities to crude binaries.

PART IV

LONG COVID AND YOM KIPPUR

Chapter 14

FASTING AND LONG COVID – Introduction

In late summer, a woman experiencing serious long-term COVID symptoms asked me to publicly address the implications of her condition for fasting on Yom Kippur.

Investigation confirmed the need for a public response; I kept meeting people who were afraid that rabbis would either dismiss their illness, or else ask only whether their doctor would say that fasting might kill them. Some of those people planned to eat anyway, but had lost confidence in and respect for ordinary halakhic processes; some of them planned to fast, despite knowing that this would have serious and sustained adverse health consequences.

You'll find my public responsum in Part 6 of this series, which were published weekly before Rosh HaShannah. I think reading them has value both as pure Talmud Torah and as offering insight into how psak is refined from the raw source material (whether or not one thinks I did it properly, or reached the correct result. I've edited the essays slightly and inserted a few comments to make the overall product more coherent.)

Here are the questions I started with: ZZ   x

1) Must a medical fact-pattern be a potential proximate cause of death to fall under the rubric of *pikuach nefesh*? For example: Is it *pikuach nefesh* to prevent a 30-year-old from developing a cardiac condition that will make them significantly more vulnerable to fatal heart disease, but only after they turn 60?

2) How does halakhah relate to medical fact-patterns that have only recently emerged, and therefore whose long-term effects (if any) simply cannot be known at this time?

Mishnah Yoma 82a states:

A *choleh* (=ill person; the Hebrew neuter translates into English as masculine) –
we feed him (on Yom Kippur) at the direction of *beki'in*/experts:
If no *beki'in* are present –
we feed him at his own direction, until he says "Enough".

The mishnah does not specify how ill a *choleh* must be, in other words it does not define the halakhic **standard** to permit eating. The plain meaning of the Mishnah appears to be that the question of whether this *choleh* meets the standard of illness necessary to make eating permissible is best determined by experts, although the *choleh*'s subjective opinion is sufficient when no experts are available.

However, Rabbi Yannai on Talmud Yoma 83a offers a very different interpretation:

אמר רבי ינאי:
חולה אומר צריך,
ורופא אומר אינו צריך –
שומעין לחולה,
מאי טעמא? לב יודע מרת נפשו.
פשיטא?!
מהו דתימא? רופא קים ליה טפי –
קא משמע לן.
Said Rabbi Yannai:
If the *choleh* says "I need (to eat),
but the *rofei* (=doctor) says "He does not need" –
we heed the *choleh*.
Why? *The heart knows the bitterness of its soul* (Mishlei 14:10).
This is too obvious to bother saying!?
What would I have said? That *rofei kym lay tfay*[5] -
this teaches us otherwise.

---

[5] (approx. "the doctor knows better")

רופא אומר צריך
– וחולה אומר אינו צריך
שומעין לרופא.
מאי טעמא - תונבא הוא דנקיט ליה
If the *rofei* says: "He needs (to eat)",
but the *choleh* says "I don't need" –
we heed the *rofei*.
Why? (The *choleh*) has been taken by a stupor.

The simplest reading of Rabbi Yannai is that the *choleh* himself or herself is best equipped to determine whether he or she is ill enough to permit eating on Yom Kippur. The Mishnah's preference for expert direction therefore relates to what and how to eat, not whether to eat. However, a doctor's opinion can also justify a leniency, even when it contradicts the *choleh*, owing to the risk that illness may affect the *choleh*'s ability to realize the seriousness of their own condition.

On this understanding, neither the Mishnah nor Rabbi Yannai provides any information about the **standard** for eating.

However, our text here is surprisingly inelegant. Experienced readers of Talmud would expect the reasons for and analysis of the first and second parts of Rabbi Yannai's statement to be literarily parallel. Instead, the first half's rationale is a verse from Proverbs, whereas the second's is formulated in colloquial Aramaic; and the first rationale is challenged as making the statement *peshitta*, whereas the second is not.

One manuscript (Munich 6; other ms. have parts of this addition; see the Friedberg Jewish Manuscript Society website) inserts a parallel *peshitta* challenge and response to the second rationale.

רופא אומר צריך

וחולה אומר אינו צריך –

שומעין לרופא.

מאי טעמא - תונבא הוא דנקיט ליה

פשיטא?!

מהו דתימא?

חולה קים ליה טפי -

קא משמע לן

ספק נפשות להקל

If the doctor says: "He needs (to eat)",

but the *choleh* says "I don't need" –

we heed the doctor.

Why? He has been taken by a stupor.

This is too obvious to bother saying!?

What would I have said?

That the ill person *kym lay tfay* –

this teaches us otherwise,

that in cases of *safek nefashot* one must rule leniently.

Safek nefashot is generally understood to mean that there is some chance that the issue is life-or-death. (Note also that the phrase *safek nefashot lehakel* appears directly after the rationale "He has been taken by a stupor" in several other manuscripts, with no intervening *peshitta* challenge.) So this version suggests that the standard for being fed on Yom Kippur is an illness with some chance of being fatal.

A quite different version of the text was available to a medieval halakhist whose first name was likely Yitzchak, and to Rabbeinu Tam, as attested (with variations) in Or Zarua, Mordekhai, Rosh, Hagahot Maimoniot, Tosafot Yeshanim, and Tosafot HaRosh, and cited by Beit Yosef. This version replaces the *peshitta* challenge to the first rationale entirely, and may in fact have omitted the rationale and had the *peshitta* challenge following directly from Rabbi Yannai's statement. (The rationale is also omitted in several Talmud manuscripts. As it appears in a similar structure later in the sugya, one can easily argue that it was accidentally moved up by a copyist.)

אמר רבי ינאי:

חולה אומר צריך,

ורופא אומר אינו צריך –

שומעין לחולה,

מאי טעמא? לב יודע מרת נפשו.

פשיטא?! ספק נפשות הוא?!

מהו דתימא?

איבעותי מיבעית, סבר אי לא אכיל, **מיית** -

קא משמע לן

Said Rabbi Yannai:

If the *choleh* says "I need (to eat),

but the doctor says "He does not need" –

we heed the *choleh*.

Why? *The heart knows the bitterness of its soul* (Mishlei 14:10).

This is too obvious to bother saying!? It is a case of *safek nefashot*!?

What would I have said?

He is terrified, thinking that if he doesn't eat, he will die -

this teaches us otherwise.

This version seems to explicitly assign the case as one in which the *choleh* claims to have a possibly fatal illness. That is how Rabbeinu Tam's interlocutor read it.

Rabbeinu Tam read it very differently. Here is the report of his position in Or Zarua (Laws of Yom Kippur) Section 280:

וְלִישְׁנָא דְ"מַיִּת" אַל יִטְעָךְ -
שֶׁכֵּן לְשׁוֹן הַתַּלְמוּד;
דְּאָ"כ דְּדַיְּקַתְּ לִישְׁנָא,
מַאי "סְפֵק נְפָשׁוֹת הִיא"!?
אֶלָּא, הַאי "מַיִּת" =
שֶׁמִּתְיָרֵא לַחֲלוֹת וּלְקַלְקֵל

Let the language "he will die" not mislead you—
as that is (just) the way of Talmudic language;
as if your close reading was correct,
why would the Talmud describe this as *safek nefashot*!?
Rather, "he will die" =
that he is afraid lest he become ill and deteriorate.

Rabbeinu Tam offers this reading in support of his practical legal ruling, directly opposing Rabbi Yitzchak, that the *choleh* can eat on the basis of claimed illness even without claiming that the illness is potentially fatal.

One might understand Rabbeinu Tam as relating only to the *choleh*'s **claim**, but that observers must still conclude that the *choleh* is **describing** a potentially fatal illness. However, this does not seem a plausible interpretation of (what may be) Rabbeinu Tam's position as presented by Rabbeinu Asher (Yoma 8:13):

וַאֲפִילוּ לַסְּפָרִים שֶׁכָּתוּב בָּהֶן
"אִי לָא אֲכִילְנָא, מַיְּיתְנָא" –
אֵין לִלְמוֹד מִזֶּה דְּדַוְקָא עַל סְפֵק מִיתָה מַאֲכִילִין,
דְּלִישְׁנָא דְ"מַיְּיתְנָא" - לָאו דַּוְקָא,
אֶלָּא שֶׁדֶּרֶךְ הַחוֹלֶה לוֹמַר כֵּן מֵחֲמַת פַּחַד מִיתָה
Even according to the mss. which have written in them
"If I don't eat, I will die"—
one should not learn from this that we feed someone only when
there is a *safek* of death,
because the language "I will die" is not intended rigorously,
rather it is the way of a *choleh* to say that out of fear of death.

Rosh clearly understands (the position that may be) Rabbeinu Tam as permitting a *choleh* to eat on Yom Kippur even when there is objectively no *safek* that fasting will cause death.

The obvious problem is that Rabbeinu Tam must have **some** standard other than mere illness to permit eating on Yom Kippur. Moreover, why should the standard for eating on Yom Kippur be different than for violating other prohibitions, such as those of Shabbat, where it seems clear that we require the *choleh* to be *yesh bo sakkanah* ="dangerously ill"?!

Rav Shaul David Botschko shlita cites[6] (his father Rav Mosheh z"l's brilliant solution to the second question. Rav Mosheh Botschko argued that the Torah does not directly prohibit "eating" on Yom Kippur; rather, it obligates one to "afflict one's soul" by fasting. He further pointed out that at least one other required "affliction" on Yom Kippur, that of not-washing, creates a prohibition that is conditional rather than absolute: only washing-of-pleasure (*rechitzah shel ta'anug*) is prohibited, and one is therefore permitted to wash for the purpose of removing unpleasant things from one's skin. Perhaps, then – even though everyone agrees that the prohibition against eating and drinking is more severe than the one against washing, and even according to those who hold that all the afflictions are *deoraita*, and even though everyone agrees that the general standard for violating a Biblical prohibition (including those against eating) is *safek nefashot* – the prohibition against eating on Yom Kippur similarly applies only to eating that removes affliction. Eating in response to serious illness, even when the illness is not potentially fatal, might be the equivalent of washing-not-of-pleasure.

I have loved each of the (too few) ideas I've so far read in the name of Rav Mosheh Botschko, and I'm also greatly enjoying and immensely benefiting from the recent privilege of corresponding with Rav Shaul David, and of learning more of his Torah. But even if I became

---

[6] http://www.toraisrael.com/lesson.asp?id=2156)

convinced that this was Rabbeinu Tam's intent, and/or that the Shulchan Arukh rules in accordance with this understanding of Rabbeinu Tam, and that it has legs in contemporary halakhah – I would still need to develop a clear standard for when eating is permitted, and in what amounts.

Chapter 15

FASTING and LONG COVID - Part 2

Vayikra 18:5 states that

You must keep my chukim and mishpatim that a person must do
(=asher yaaseh otam hoadam)
and live by them (=vochai bohem).

Talmud Yoma 85b derives that

one should chai by them – and not die by them.

However, this derivation does not apply to all *chukim* and *mishpatim*. Implicitly, there are commands that a person must do even if they lead to death.

Three sins famously are *yehareg v'al ya'avor*, meaning that Jews are obligated to die rather than actively transgress them. That list can be expanded somewhat, for example to include commands that entail warfare, but the clear implication is that to preserve one's life (and consensus halakhah extends this to others' lives), one may or must violate all Torah mitzvot not on the list.

The general halakhic term for preserving life is *pikuach nefesh*. Halakhah generally treats *safek pikuach nefesh* as the equivalent of *pikuach nefesh* (and generally sets a very low bar in the realm of *pikuach nefesh* as to the probability necessary to be considered a *safek*). *Safek pikuach nefesh* is therefore **sufficient** to permit violations of all mitzvot that are not *yehareg v'al ya'avor*.

It does not follow that *safek pikuach nefesh* is **necessary** to permit **any** such violations.

We saw in Part 1 that ROSH permits eating on Yom Kippur in situations that fall short of *safek pikuach nefesh*. ROSH (Yoma 8:13) states that

> Even according to the manuscripts that have written in them "If I don't eat, I will die" – one should not learn from this that we feed someone only when there is a *safek* of death"

.

My conclusion was that "Rosh clearly understands Rabbeinu Tam as permitting a *choleh* to eat on Yom Kippur even when there is objectively no *safek* that fasting will cause death".

Yehuda Gale corrected my assumption that ROSH is channeling Rabbeinu Tam rather than offering his own position. The truth is that ROSH makes no mention of Rabbeinu Tam, nor does he quote the colorful rhetoric attributed to Rabbeinu Tam on this subject: ("Are ill people prophets?!").

Yehuda also correctly noted that Rabbeinu Tam, as cited by Hagahot Mordekhai Shabbat 463, Or Zarua Hilkhot Yom Kippurim 280, and Hagahot Maimoniot Hilkhot Shevitut Asor 2:5, explicitly frames his standard as permitting violations of Shabbat as well as of Yom Kippur. His position therefore cannot be explained the rationale we cited from Rav Mosheh Botschko z"l's for why eating on Yom Kippur could uniquely be permitted at a standard below *safek pikuach nefesh*.

ROSH himself does not mention Shabbat, and the citation of Rabbeinu Tam in Recanati 266 also doesn't mention Shabbat. So Rav Botschko's explanation can explain ROSH, and perhaps that was also Rabbeinu Tam's true position. However, Beit Yosef OC 618 conflates ROSH's position with that of Rabbeinu Tam as brought in Hagahot Maimoniot, which does mention Shabbat. It therefore seems unlikely that post-Shulchan Arukh halakhah developed on the basis of a claim that the lower standard applied only to eating on Yom Kippur and not to violating Shabbat.

Let us therefore assume that ROSH and Rabbeinu Tam, and Beit Yosef, allow violation of all non-*yehareg v'al ya'avor* prohibitions even when there is objectively no *safek* that observing them will cause death. What is their standard for permitting such violations, and how do they derive that standard?

A possible derivation appears in a 1935 responsum written to the Sridei Eish by the Kozhilglover Rav, the Holocaust martyr Rabbi Aryeh Tzvi Frommer. While developing his position on the kashrut of animals that are stunned before shechitah, Rabbi Frommer states:

על כן נראה לענ"ד

דהראב"ד ז"ל נחית לדברינו הנ"ל

דמסוכן הוא חיות בלתי שלם,

וכיון דלא חשיב חי –

הוא ג"כ בכלל הדרשא

ד"*וחי בהם* - ולא שיסתכן בהם",

וע"כ לא צריך ספק מיתה כלל!

כל שהוא בגדר מסוכן –

מאכילין אותו לשוב להיות בגדר חי

It therefore seems in my humble opinion

that the RAAVAD z"l reached our opinion above

that to be a מסוכן/*mesukan*/endangered is to be incompletely alive,

and since the *mesukan* is not considered חי/alive,

the *mesukan* is also included in the midrash halakhah

that "*one must live by them* – and not be endangered by them".

Therefore, there is no need of a *safek* of death at all!

Anyone in the category of *mesukan* –

we feed him so as to return him to being within the category "*chai*".

I am not aware of any prior or subsequent halakhic authority explicitly making this argument within the derivation from *vochai bohem*. But regardless, Rabbi Frommer provides us with potential language for the standard we are seeking approach – a person can be *mesukan*/endangered without being in a "*safek* of death", and one can violate Shabbat or Yom Kippur in order to remove a person from the status of *mesukan*, or (presumably) in order to prevent them from reaching that state.

Is there evidence for a halakhically significant status of *mesukan* distinct from that of *safek nefashot*? Is there evidence that *mesukan* is the correct standard for permitting violations of Shabbat and Yom Kippur? The full citation of ROSH provides very strong evidence for both these claims. ROSH writes as follows:

כתבו התוספות:

- הא דקאמר הש"ס "חולה אומר צריך אני"

היינו שאומר שהוא ירא שאם לא יאכל – שיכביד, ויהיה מסוכן למות.

ויש ספרים שכתוב בהן [בתר] מילתא דרבי ינאי

"פשיטא?! ספק נפשות להקל?!

מהו דתימא? האי דקאמר חולה 'צריך אני' - בעותי הוא דקא מבעית; סבר: אי לא אכילנא, מיתנא.

קא משמע לן.

אלמא דוקא משום ספק מיתה מאכילין אותו

עד כאן.

ונראה לי

דחומרא גדולה היא זאת בספק

דאין לך רופא שיאמר 'אם לא יאכל - שמא ימות'

אלא הרופא דרכו לומר 'אם לא יאכל - אפשר שיכביד חליו ויסתכן'.

ואפי' לספרים שכתוב בהן 'אי לא אכילנא מיתנא'

אין ללמוד מזה דדוקא על ספק מיתה מאכילין, דלישנא דמיתנא לאו דוקא, אלא שדרך החולה לומר כן מחמת פחד המיתה.

The Tosafists write:
"When the Talmud says 'the *choleh* says: I need to be fed' -
it means that he is afraid that if he doesn't eat - his illness will intensify, and he will be *mesukan lamut* (= in danger of death).
There are (also) manuscripts in which it is written [after] the statement of Rabbi Yannai:

"That is too obvious to bother saying! *Safek nefashot lehakel*?!

What would I have said? That when the *choleh* says 'I need (to be fed)'
– they are (merely) being terrified, thinking that if they don't eat, they
will die –
So (Rabbi Yannai's statement) teaches us that this is not so.'
So it seems that it is only because if a *safek* of death that we feed (the
choleh)."
This ends Tosafot's words.
But it seems to me that this is a great stringency in the matter of *safek*,
because you will not find a doctor who will say 'if (the *choleh*) does not
eat, maybe he will die';
rather, the way of the doctor is to say 'if (the *choleh*) does not eat, his
illness may intensify and he will be endangered/*yistaken*'.
Even according to the manuscripts in which is written "If I don't eat - I
will die",
one should not learn from this that we feed (the *choleh*) only when
there is a *safek* of death,
because the language "I will die" is not intended rigorously, rather it is
the way of the *choleh* to say this out of fear of death.

ROSH thus distinguishes between the statements "maybe he will
die" and "I will die" on the one hand, and "his illness may intensify and
he will be endangered/*yistaken*" on the other. This exactly parallels
Rabbi Frommer, and sets *sakkanah*/endangerment as the proper
standard for allowing eating on Yom Kippur. ROSH is cited by Beit
Yosef and codified in Shulchan Arukh OC 638:1.However, while
sakkanah is clearly different than *safek nefashot*, it's not clear what it
means.

One possible source for the category is Tractate Gittin chapter 6.
Mishnah Gittin 6:5 records the position of R. Shimon Shezuri that if a
mesukan orders someone to write a get for his wife, without saying
"write and give it", one can nonetheless give it to the wife so that she is
actually divorced, as this is considered "a command given in
contemplation of death". The Yerushalmi cites a beraita that says the
same is true of a *choleh*, then comments:

מה בין מסוכן מה בין חולה?
חולה - כדרך הארץ;
ומסוכן - כל שקפץ עליו החולי.

What is the difference between a *mesukan* and an (ordinary) *choleh*?
A *choleh* – in the ordinary way;
a *mesukan* – one who had the illness "jump on him"

Rambam Hilkhot Gerushin 2:12 expands on the Yerushalmi:

מסוכן,
והוא אדם שקפץ עליו החולי במהרה
והכביד חליו מיד[7]

The *mesukan*,
he being a person whom the illness jumped upon rapidly
and intensified the illness for him immediately.

ROSH Gittin 7:15 quotes the Yerushalmi. ROSH Berakhot 2:15 and Yoma 8:1 also state that because washing on Yom Kippur is *derabanan*, one can wash for anything that is medicinal even if not for a *sakkanah*; the implication is that the standard for violating a *deoraita is sakkanah*.

So perhaps a *mesukan* is anyone whose illness intensifies rapidly, and one can eat or drink on Yom Kippur to prevent such an intensification, even though there is no short-term risk that one will die as the result of failure to eat or drink. Such intensification is also the standard for violating Shabbat and other transgressions which are not *yehareg v'al ya'avor*.

But even if one accepts this argument fully, we still need a definition, or at least a diagnostic, of what sort of intensification of what sort of illness is necessary to permit non-fasting.

---

[7] cf. Rambam Hilkhot Zekhiyyah uMatonoh 8:24: והמסוכן, והוא שקפץ עליו החולי והכביד עליו חליו

Chapter 16

FASTING AND LONG COVID - Part 3

The halakhic principle *safek nefashot lehakel* is generally understood to mean "Where there is doubt regarding danger to human life, protect human life even if that requires violating halakhic prohibitions (other than those one must die before violating)".

"*Safek*" in most halakhic contexts refers exclusively to 50/50 scenarios. Even 51/49 generate a *rov*/majority, and halakhah treats the more likely scenario as true. Rabbinic law often requires that the less-likely scenario not be a *miut hamtzui*, usually set somewhere between 5-15%. But 96/4 odds are certainly good enough to invoke *rov*.

The problem is that another halakhic principle states that "*ein holkhin b'fikuach nefesh achar harov*", which is understood to mean that one can violate halakhah even to protect against a one in a thousand chance of human death, and perhaps even one in a million. So which is it, *safek lehakel* or *ein holkhin achar harov*?

One resolution references another halakhic context in which *safek* may mean "any chance at all", namely *mamzerut*. Igrot Mosheh EH 4:17 argues that Halakhah generally accepts statistically projected majorities (*ruba d'leta kaman*) heuristically, to make decisions in cases of *safek*. But in contexts that have a specific rule governing cases of *safek*, such as "(the Torah means) a definite *mamzer*, not a *safek mamzer*", statistically projected majorities are irrelevant.

"*And live by them* - and not die by them" therefore means that statistically projected majorities are irrelevant to cases of *safek nefashot*. Regarding *mamzerut* and *pikuach nefesh*, then, *safeik X lehakel* and *ein holkhin b'X achar harov* both require accounting for extremely unlikely cases.

Rav Moshe notes that formal majorities are different. For example, if experience has shown that most cows in the world are kosher, then any cow one meets can be treated as kosher – that is a statistically projected majority. But if two definitely treyf cows and one definitely kosher cow are in an enclosure, and we cannot know which is which, and one cow emerges – that cow is treyf because of a formal majority. Similarly, if two definite mamzers and one uncertain mamzer are in an enclosure, and we cannot know which is which, and one person emerges – that person is a definite mamzer. So too, if two healthy people and one deathly ill person are in an enclosure, and we cannot know which is which, and one person emerges – one cannot violate *deoraita* halakhah in order to treat that person.

In practice, the task of a competent posek in such cases is to find reasonable arguments for transforming formal majorities into statistically projected majorities. Anyone using formal majorities to rule that a specific person is a mamzer, or to forbid treating a specific patient, is probably demonstrating incompetence. Yet I think the formal rules serve the purpose of preventing people from trampling all of Halakhah in the name of *pikuach nefesh*, or from regarding sexual sin as without consequences.

This interplay between formalism and common sense may be at the core of the Talmudic discussion regarding feeding the ill on Yom Kippur. Talmud Yoma 83a reads as follows:

(TEXT) Said Rabbi Yannai:
"If the ill person says "Need", but the doctor says "Does not need" – we heed the ill person ...
If the doctor says "Needs" but the ill person says "Don't need" – we heed the doctor ..."
(CHALLENGE) But the Mishnah says: "An ill person – we feed them at the direction of experts."
(This implies)
At the directions of "experts", but not at his own direction!?
At the direction of "experts", but not at the direction of a single expert (which contradicts the first half of Rabbi Yannai's statement)!?
(RESOLUTION) What case are we dealing with here (in the Mishnah)?
One in which the ill person said: "I don't need"
(while in Rabbi Yannai's case, the ill person says "Need").

(CHALLENGE) Still, why not feed the ill person at the direction of a single expert!?

(RESOLUTION) Because (the Mishnah's case is one in which) another expert is present and saying "Doesn't need".

(TEXT of MISHNAH) "We feed him at the direction of experts."

(CHALLENGE) "This is too obvious to say (even when the ill person and one expert say "Doesn't need")!? It is a case of *safek nefashot*, and *safek nefashot lehakel*!?

(RESOLUTION) It is necessary to say, because the case is that two other experts are present and saying "Doesn't need". Even though Rav Safra said that two witnesses equal one hundred, and vice versa – those words apply only to testimony, but with regard to estimation - we follow the majority of minds; but – those words apply only with regard to estimation in financial cases, but here – it is *safek nefashot*, (and so we apply Rav Safra's rule).

(CHALLENGE) But the end of the Mishnah reads: "If no experts are present – we feed him at his own direction", which implies that the beginning of the Mishnah ("An ill person – we feed him at the direction of experts") is also a case in which he said: "Need" (meaning that we don't feed a patient who says "Need" without expert corroboration)!?

(RESOLUTION) The Mishnah's text is lacking, and must be paraphrased to mean the following:

'Regarding what case were the words "one feeds an ill person at the direction of experts" (implying not at the direction of a single expert) said?

When (the ill person) said: "I don't need" (and a single expert agreed); But if (the ill person) said: "I need" – then if there aren't two experts present (saying "Doesn't need"), rather only one saying "Doesn't need" – we feed (the ill person) at his own direction (despite the opinion of the single expert, as Rabbi Yannai said).

(CONTRARY OPINION) Mar bar Rav Ashi said:

"Whenever the ill person says "I need" – even if there are one hundred (experts) saying "Doesn't need" – we heed (the ill person),

as Scripture says: *The heart knows the bitterness of its own soul.*

Here is my paraphrase:

Rabbi Yannai states that when doctor and patient disagree, we heed whichever one says that eating on Yom Kippur is necessary. This suggests that any possibility of danger is sufficient to permit eating! The Talmud responds that Rabbi Yannai allows us to heed a doctor's claim of danger over the patient's denial only when no doctor is supporting the patient. If a doctor supports the patient, then it is two (doctor plus patient) against one (doctor), and majority rules, and we may not feed the patient.

What about *safek nefashot lehakel*?

That applies only when opinions are split 50/50.

What if there are two doctors on each side? Does the patient's opinion win because majority rules?

No, because two are formally counted as equal to infinity, so this is formally a 50/50 split.

But don't two count as infinity only when they are formally testifying, not when giving opinions?

No, only in financial cases; with regard to *nefashot*, they count as infinity even when offering opinions, so this is formally a 50/50 split, and *safek nefashot lehakel*.

What if the patient says "need", and is opposed by two doctors? Shouldn't that be two against one, and therefore we may not feed the patient?

Yes, if one considers the patient and the doctors as "in the same enclosure". That's Rabbi Yannai's view. Mar bar Rav Ashi disagrees, because their opinions are derived via different epistemologies. Mar bar Rav Ashi holds that majority is irrelevant whenever the patient says "Need".

The upshot is that the Talmud leaves only one case in which the conclusion is that we don't feed the patient. That case is when the single doctor who says "Needs" is opposed by the patient and another doctor.

But the practical solution to that case is obvious – bring in more doctors until a second one says "Needs"! Since two witnesses have the same credibility as any larger number, the result will then be a *safek*, and *safek nefashot lehakel*.

However, Maimonides (as explained by Maggid Mishneh) understood Mar bar Rav Ashi as completely rejecting the application of "two equals infinity" to opinions. Maimonides therefore follows the majority of medical advice whenever the patient doesn't declare a need to eat.

However, Maimonides also introduces an antidemocratic variable – some doctors are more expert than others. Furthermore, some rishonim note that with regard to some common conditions, experienced laypeople may count as experts. The result is that if one is convinced that it is absolutely necessary, one can always feed the patient, but if one is not convinced, and the patient is also not convinced, one need not always feed the patient.

All the above assumes that *safek nefashot lehakel* and *ein holkhin b'fikuach nefesh achar harov* mean the same thing. But we saw in Part 2 that the halakhic standard for violating prohibitions, and perhaps especially for eating on *Yom Kippur*, is formulated not as *safek nefashot* but rather as *efshar lavo liydei sakkanah* =the situation may become dangerous. So an alternate resolution is that *ein holkhin b'fikuach nefesh achar harov* applies to cases of informally defined probability, such as deciding which medical opinion to accept; whereas *safek nefashot lehakel* applies in contexts where probability is formally defined (e.g. we know that X of the people in a specific room have been poisoned, but not which, and administering the antidote requires an *additional* deoraita violation of Shabbat for each person, e.g. grinding a subjectively adjusted mixture of herbs.) My sense is that this resolution will yield roughly the same bottom line as the ones above.

However, this entire discussion has been about the opinions of *cholim* (=ill people) and *beki'in* (=experts). One might argue that people cannot simply declare themselves *cholim*; maybe a *baki* needs to declare you a *choleh* before your opinion matters at all. Conversely, maybe doctors count as *beki'in* only when dealing with conditions with which the medical profession has extensive experience. With regard to new diseases, perhaps there are no *beki'in*.

Chapter 17

FASTING AND LONG COVID - Part 4

People for whom fasting on Yom Kippur is dangerous are often told to drink or eat "shiurim". The point of this ironically named strategy is to NOT eat the *shiur* that renders one liable for *karet*. (The *shiurim* for eating and drinking on Yom Kippur are defined as amounts consumed within a set time.)

Conventional analysis distinguishes between halakhot that are *dechuyah* with regard to *pikuach nefesh*, and those that are *hutrah*. A *dechuyah* halakhah may be violated only to the extent necessary to save a life, whereas a *hutrah* halakhah simply doesn't apply in the context of lifesaving. So the requirement of "shiurim" apparently demonstrates that eating on Yom Kippur is *dechuyah* rather than *hutrah*. A Soloveitchik tradition reports that Rav Chaim Brisker ruled *hutrah* and never recommended shiurim.[8]

On this understanding, "shiurim" is <u>always</u> a strategy rather than a psak. The underlying psak for anyone told to eat "shiurim" is that they can and must eat any amount necessary to avoid any risk defined as *pikuach nefesh*.

Rav Shaul Dovid Botschko shlita suggests a way that "shiurim" can be understood as a psak, meaning that some people are permitted to eat less than a *shiur* (=*chatzi shiur*) even though their medical condition would not justify violating the *karet* prohibition, and even though we rule like Rav Yochanan that *chatzi shiur* is a Torah prohibition. This position seems explicit in Sefer HaChinnukh (Emor #313):

with less than (these amounts) –
there is no *karet* prohibition, rather this is like a *chatzi shiur*.

---

[8]See Part 5 for a revised account of this tradition. I've left the position here as originally written for the sake of the analysis.

Therefore, someone who is ill,
even though not in <u>a complete danger/*sakkanah g'murah*</u>,
if he is very weak –
it is proper to feed him and give him to drink little by little.

It seems that "complete danger" is needed to permit eating a full *shiur*, whereas "incomplete danger" suffices to permit eating *chatzi shiur*. However, Minchat Chinnukh (note 5) comments:

It seems from the words of the rabbi/author (of Sefer HaChinnukh)
that there is a distinction between the (full) shiur,
which one feeds only in a context of danger,
and less than a shiur,
which one feeds even in a context where there is no danger.
But the truth is that I have not seen this distinction made anywhere,
as certainly no Torah prohibition is permitted
where there is no danger . . .
One can impose this meaning on the language of the rabbi/author,
but his words are a little confused

Minchat Chinnukh sees Sefer HaChinnukh's position, as he understands it, as unprecedented. However, Rav Botschko points to Tosafot Shavuot 23b. Talmud Shavuot 23b wonders how a Mishnah can state that an oath not to eat forbidden foods is binding, when
a. redundant oaths are not binding, and
b. all oaths not to violate prohibitions are redundant, because all Jews are considered sworn to obey them since Sinai?!
Resh Lakish responds that the Mishnah is discussing a case of *chatzi shiur*, while Rav Yochanan offers a different solution. The Talmud's offers a very weak explanation for why Rav Yochanan rejects Resh Lakish's solution. Tosafot ask: Why didn't the Talmud instead explain that Rav Yochanan's rejection of Resh Lakish's response stems from their disagreement about *chatzi shiur*, namely that Rav Yochanan holds

that *chatzi shiur* is Biblically prohibited, and therefore oaths not to violate via *chatzi shiur* are redundant?! Tosafot answer:

> since this is only a 'mere prohibition' –
> it is not considered sworn from Sinai . . .
> Even though (the principle that "Torah prohibitions do not apply redundantly", which can be understood as a special case of 'sworn from Sinai',) means that prohibitions phrased by the Torah as DON'Ts don't apply when redundant with prohibitions phrased as DOs (which implies that even prohibitions phrased as Dos are 'sworn from Sinai')
>
> . . .
>
> Nonetheless, *chatzi shiur*, which lacks even a DO,
> rather is just a mere prohibition/*issur b'alma* –
> is not considered 'sworn from Sinai'.

I cannot at this point make sense of the position that some Torah prohibitions are not be 'sworn from Sinai'. Nor do I have any idea where the boundary is between those prohibitions that are 'sworn' and those that are 'not sworn', nor how to tell which is which, except that those punished by *karet* are 'sworn'. I don't know why 'not sworn' Torah prohibitions may be violated at a standard lower than *pikuach nefesh*. Regardless, the existence of Tosafot's position makes it likely that Chinnukh should be taken at face value as allowing a *chatzi shiur* at a lower standard than is necessary to permit a full *shiur*.

(Rav Botschko argues that because one may opt not to fulfill a DO if the cost would be greater than 10% of one's property, and one ought not to fulfill it at a cost of greater than 20%, Tosafot's standard for violating *chatzi shiur* must be lower than "health damage that you would pay 20% of your property to prevent". However, it seems to me that this depends on whether that principle applies to prohibitions derived from DOs. See e.g. Mishneh Berurah OC 656:9 for an indication that the relevant axis is passive vs. active rather than DO vs. DON'T.)

I have additional evidence for the existence of a position that the standard of "danger" necessary to permit a Torah prohibition varies with the severity of the prohibition.

Talmud Ketubot 61a relays a series of anecdotes:

> Said Rav Anan bar Tachalifa:
> I was standing before Mar Shmuel, and they brought him a mushroom stew,
> and had he not given me (some to eat) – I would have been endangered/*istakani*.
> Said Rav Ashi:
> I was standing before Rav Kehana,
> and they brought him turnip slices in vinegar,
> and had he not given me (some to eat) –
> I would have been endangered/ *istakani* . . .

The context of these stories is an obligation to allow waiters to serve themselves before serving foods that induce cravings. One might therefore dismiss the word "endangered" as hyperbole, especially as all the food involved was kosher. But the last story in the series undercuts any such dismissal:

Ameimar and Mar Zutra and Rav Ashi were sitting at the entrance to King Izgur's palace.
The king's seneschal passed by (carrying food for the king).
Rav Ashi say Mar Zutra's face turn white. He took (some of the king's food) with his fingers and put it on (Mar Zutra's) mouth.
The (seneschal) said to Rav Ashi: You have destroyed the king's meal!?
The (guards) said to (Rav Ashi): Why did you do this?
He replied to them: A dish prepared like this is not fit for the king.
They said: Why?
He said: I saw "something else" (Rashi: meat from a leprous pig) in it.
They checked and did not find anything.

(Rav Ashi) took their fingers and put them on one piece. He said:
Did you check this one?
(A miracle occurred for him) and they found it in that piece.
The Rabbis said to Rav Ashi: Why did you rely on a miracle?
He said to them: I saw a spirit of leprosy/*ruach tzora'at* spreading
over (Mar Zutra).

Here the food is presumably not kosher, and yet Rav Ashi feeds it to
Mar Zutra. So the "danger" involved must be great enough to permit
violating a Torah prohibition. Is this sort of craving a threat to life in
the sense of *pikuach nefesh*? More likely "danger/*sakkanah*" here
means something short of a threat to life, and yet Rav Ashi fed Mar
Zutra.

One might argue that these stories are *aggada* rather than
halakahah. But RIF and ROSH both cite Rav Anan bar Tachalifa!

One might still argue that they cite him specifically in the context
of obligations toward waiters. But Korban Netanel and many other
rishonim reject this:

RIF and ROSH cite this story to teach us that this situation is a
sakkanah for him,
and he is treated like a pregnant woman who has smelled
(something that induces cravings),
as (the obligation to feed those who smell crave-inducing food)
applies not only to waiters but to anyone.

The remaining question is whether this sort of craving represents
the standard for violating all Torah prohibitions, or only some.
Rabbeinu Manoach, commenting on Rambam Hilkhot Shevitut Asor
2:9, cites R. Yitzchak b'R. Avraham citing the story of Rav Ashi and
Mar Zutra, then comments:

There are those who say that they were lenient only with
regard to a DON'T prohibition (not having a specific

punishment) and (in such cases) the Sages equated the law of a
pregnant woman who smelled (and developed a craving) with
that of a healthy man who smelled (and developed a craving),
but that with regard to a *karet* prohibition, such as here –
we only feed a pregnant woman who has cravings,
because it is ordinary for her to be endangered when she smells
a food but does not eat it,
but a healthy man, if he smells on Yom Kippur –
we don't feed him,
as he is obligated to settle his mind.
It is good to be strict about this because of the tricksters.
This seems to be the position of Rambam . . .

Rabbeinu Manoach has no uniform standard for violating Torah
prohibitions; rather, it depends on their severity. Minchat Chinnukh's
incredulity therefore seems overstated. The position that the standard
for eating a *chatzi shiur* is lower than that for eating a full *shiur* cannot
be summarily dismissed. One might even argue that the best way to
read the story is that Rav Ashi fed Mar Zutra only a *chatzi shiur*.

Chapter 18

FASTING and LONG COVID - Part 5

Earwitnesses report that Rav Chaim Brisker claimed never to have instructed a dangerously ill person to limit their eating on Yom Kippur to 'shiurim'. He also emphasized the importance of this psak to his son and successor R. Moshe Soloveitchik. In PART 4, I used this tradition to illustrate the position that eating on Yom Kippur is "*hutrah*" rather than "*dechuyah*" with regard to *pikuach nefesh*, meaning that so long as a situation is defined as *pikuach nefesh*, there is no prohibition of eating.

SBM alum Rabbi David Fried challenged my presentation of Rav Chaim:

"What I was always taught by 'my rebbeim is that Rav Chaim distinguished between when there's actually sakkanat nefashot right now, and when a person needs to eat to prevent an underlying condition from potentially worsening into a situation of *sakkanat nefashot*, and only in the former would 'shiurim' not apply."

Rabbi Fried's version is confirmed by Chiddushei Maran RYZ HaLevi (CMRYZH) to Rambam Shevitut Asor 2:8. (See also the other report of Rav Chaim's position in Hamoadim baHalakhah p.82; I am not fully convinced this distinction was Rav Chaim's.) CMRYZH explains the position as follows:

If a person *is* deathly ill, we treat the person and not the disease – anything that improves the patient's health diminishes the risk of death,
and eating full shiurim is always better for their overall health than eating 'shiurim'.
However,
if the person *is in danger of becoming* deathly ill,
then we violate Torah prohibitions only in order to prevent the illness,
not to treat the patient's overall condition,
and 'shiurim' are preferable.

This sounds like a conceptual distinction. However, on careful examination, Rav Chaim's contribution turns out to be purely empirical. R. Chaim held that eating full shiurim rather than 'shiurim' improved outcomes for deathly ill patients, but did not affect whether patients became deathly ill.

> "... it emerges that the entire danger is generated solely
> by prevention of eating,
> and in such a case, since this danger can also be
> prevented by 'shiurim',
> it is forbidden to feed him a full shiur'."

CMRYZ contends that this fits beautifully with Sefer HaChinnukh (#313)'s position that one may eat 'shiurim' for a condition that is less than "sakkanah gemurah".

> ובפחות מכאן - אין בו איסור כרת, אלא דינו כחצי שיעור,
> ולפיכך: מי שהוא חולה, **אף על פי שאין בו סכנה גמורה**,
> אם יהיה חלוש הרבה - ראוי להאכילו ולהשקותו מעט מעט
> "less than (these amounts) – there is no *karet* prohibition,
> rather this is like a *chatzi shiur*.
> Therefore, someone who is ill, even though not in a
> complete danger/*sakkanah g'murah*,
> if he is very weak – it is proper to feed him and give him
> to drink little by little."

CMRYZ understands this to mean that where there is only the potential of developing a fatal illness, eating "shiurim" is appropriate, **unless full shiurim are necessary to prevent the development of a potentially fatal illness**; but where potentially fatal illness is already present, one must go straight to full shiurim.

By contrast, we saw in PART 4 that Rav S. D. Botschko understands Sefer HaChinnukh to mean that without *sakkanah gemurah*, one may

never eat full shiurim. Rav Botschko therefore concludes that the case of *ein bo sakkanah gemurah* must not involve any risk of death at all.

We saw in PARTS 1-2 that according to ROSH, a *choleh* or doctor need not **claim** risk of death in order for eating to be allowed, only risk of *sakkanah*. So perhaps Sefer HaChinnukh means the objective correlate of ROSH; if neither patient nor doctor needs to claim risk of death, it follows that the situation need not actually involve "risk of death" to permit eating. On that basis, we could combine CMRYZ and Rav Botschko's readings of Sefer HaChinnukh to produce a third position, namely:

In situations that are defined as *sakkanah*, even if they don't involve actual "risk of death", one should preferably eat "shiurim", but one may eat full shiurim (or violate Shabbat) if necessary.

At first glance, this position seems a plausible match for the consensus halakhah as formulated by the Shulchan Arukh, as against Rav Chaim's position that the strategy of 'shiurim' never applies where there is present danger, and Rav Botschko's suggestion that 'shiurim' can be a *psak* rather than a strategy.

However, there are at least two compelling arguments against this position reflecting the actual halakhah.

The first is that Talmud Avodah Zarah 28b permits violating *deoraita* Shabbat prohibitions to treat various eye infections only because "the eyes connect to the heart". This implies that even the threat of blindness is not by itself sufficient to permit such violations. If blindness is not sufficient, what conditions short of death could be sufficient? (Rav Botschko might claim that this passage applies only to *deoraita* violations involving full shiurim, but our position cannot claim this.)

The second is that we have no Biblical source for allowing transgressing for the sake of health beyond life (unless we read *vachai bohem* itself broadly, as per Rav Aryeh Tzvi Frommer in PART 2).

I therefore suggest that the best way to account for all the evidence is to say that all *sakkanah* in this halakhic context involves danger to life.

However, it's very important to translate *ba liydei sakkanah* as "dangerous" rather than as "potentially fatal", for the following reason: Pikuach nefesh includes not only risk of short-term death, but also risk of earlier death. This is why poskim ban smoking. The Rabbis held – and I think reasonably so – that a period of extreme weakness or chemical imbalance could lead to constitutional damage that would shorten life expectancy. (This may yield the result that the distinction between danger to life and danger to limb has little or no practical halakhic relevance.)

It's also important to recognize that evidence of *sakkanah* can be obtained in a variety of different ways, and there can be halakhic implications from the way in which we obtain the evidence.

Way #1 = רופא אומר "צריך" – מאכילין אותו ע"פ בקיאים

A medical expert states that eating on Yom Kippur (or violating another Biblical prohibition) is necessary either to diminish a person's risk of dying from a specifically identified illness or injury, or else to prevent a condition from dangerously worsening.

ROSH's position, adopted by Shulchan Arukh, is that doctors tend to distinguish between the proximate cause of illness and the ancillary effects of fasting. Therefore a qualified doctor's statement that fasting could cause the patient's underlying condition to become dangerously worse suffices to establish risk of death, even if the doctor will not say that fasting is itself dangerous.

Way # 2 = חולה אומר "צריך אני" – מאכילין אותו ע"פ עצמו

A severely ill person declares that eating is necessary for them.

Rabbeinu Tam sharply noted that patients are not prophets. Nor are they medical experts, and furthermore, they are under enormous stress. All they can report is how they feel. Halakhah presumes that patients who say "I must eat" are reacting to internal symptoms at least equivalent to a doctor's estimation that they are at risk of developing a condition that could shorten their lives. (Note that this mode requires that the patient be diagnosed as severely ill, or else obviously so. Apparently healthy people who simply claim a need to eat cannot be **fed** by others; I'm not sure what halakhah would say about such a person feeding themselves.)

Way #3 = .עוברה שהריחה – מאכילין אותה עד שתשוב נפשה; וכן כל אדם
וכן מי שאחזו בולמוס – מאכילין אותו עד שיאירו עיניו

A person reacts to food, or presents generally, in a way that makes it clear even to nonexperts that their condition is dangerous.

We saw in PART 4 (based on Ketubot 61a) that the fact of pregnancy is not taken as halakhically significant. While pregnant women may be more likely to experience such craving, healthy men who experience cravings are given the same leeway to eat on Yom Kippur. The rule about the person seized by a *bulmus* fit reflects the same principle.

This formulation of *sakkanah* runs a serious risk of abuse and error. Rabbeinu Manoach to Shevitut Asor 2:9 writes "It is good to be strict about this because of the tricksters". Where there was actually no *sakkanah*, prohibitions may be violated accidentally or under duress. But these concerns must be balanced against Rav Chaim Soloveitchik's mantra that "I'm not being lenient about Yom Kippur; I'm being strict about *pikuach nefesh*".

The strategy called 'shiurim' is one of a group of strategies that the Talmud and subsequent Halakhah refer to under the general rubric "*hakal hakal techilah*" = the least serious violation should be violated first. These strategies often have two purposes – to minimize the prohibitions violated, and to make people less likely to sacrifice their lives as "pious fools" rather than violate prohibitions. Rav Chaim's wholesale rejection of the 'shiurim' strategy could chas veshalom backfire if a patient who would have been willing to eat small amounts now refuses to eat at all. On the other hand, ruling that a patient must try 'shiurim' first may entail a risky delay before eating as necessary.

Another halakhic strategy is called *lechishah*, whispering. This strategy is based on two narratives (Yoma 82b-83a) in which a rabbi whispers to a pregnant woman with cravings that the day is Yom Kippur. Does this strategy work when the cravings are for foods that are permanently nonkosher? Is it relevant in the same way to people who deliberately violate Shabbat? (Note that some commentators think that we are whispering to the fetus, and others that we whisper the same things to men with cravings.)

Psak should perhaps be personalized, based on which error the specific asker is more likely to commit; on the other hand, general policies play a vital role in creating the background against which people ask questions.

Chapter 19

FASTING AND LONG COVID – Part 6

Dear Rabbi Klapper,

I had COVID last November, and have been enduring "long-COVID" ever since. Thank God, I feel that overall I am improving. However, I have "flares" in which I experience fatigue, chest pain, and shortness of breath, and I cannot ever exercise for more than 10-minute increments (which more than I was able to do just a few weeks ago, and vastly more than many with long COVID). I do not take care of my children alone, and I don't read chapter books aloud to children because that causes shortness of breath. When I received my second COVID vaccine, I experienced a 3-week setback. While I have not experienced much post-exertional malaise in several months, that is probably because I have been so careful. I am very scared to test my body.

I have never been a good faster. When I fasted on Yom Kippur while nursing, it took me several days to recover even though I was otherwise healthy and spent the whole day in bed. One of the things I do to manage my illness is eating small quantities and drinking large quantities throughout the day. I fear that fasting on Yom Kippur this year would set me back for weeks at least.

Can you tell me how my situation affects my obligation to fast? I encourage you to publish a response as well. I think many people are in situations similar to mine, but either unwilling to ask or don't think there's a real question here.

With great appreciation,
Jane Doe

Dear Jane,

There is certainly a real question, and also a widespread impression that asking rabbis about it is pointless or counterproductive. I hope that my answer justifies your courage and confidence. Let me also wish you a refuah shleimah umeheirah along with all others suffering from COVID.

Here's a brief statement of what it seems medicine can say with some confidence about Long COVID: Long COVID sometimes involves measurable damage to specific organs such as the lungs or heart, but in most cases all we can identify are symptoms. Regular eating and drinking are a standard mode of mitigation symptoms, and deviations from that routine can cause regressions for an extended period of time. If patients were not hospitalized during the initial infection, there is very little chance of a relapse leading directly to death.

Therefore, if the standard for allowing eating on Yom Kippur is that fasting would significantly increase one's chance of dying in the short term, or even within the next year, then long COVID probably would not qualify for any leniency. This is true with regard to both eating normally and the strategy of "shiurim", since we rule, following Rav Yochanan against Resh Lakish (Yoma 74a and others), that eating less than the amount necessary for punishment is still Biblically prohibited, and the source for violating any Biblical prohibition is וחי בהם = "and live by them – not die by them".[9]

However, that is not the correct standard. The consensus position, articulated specifically by Rav Velvel Soloveitchik (GRYZ), is that "and live by them" applies to anything that has a halakhically significant impact on **lifespan**. Safek pikuach nefesh extends to the extremely long term.

However, there is no statistical or objective empirical basis for determining the effect on overall lifespan of a new and poorly understood condition, let alone for whether fasting will meaningfully affect that effect. We are roughly in the same scientific position as all our predecessors with regard to such conditions. Once a person is

---

[9]See however Rabbeinu Manoach to Hilkhot Shevitat Asor 2:9, who contends that the standard is lower for prohibitions that carry lesser punishments; Rav Shaul Dovid Botschko (Belkvot Hamechaber vol. 2 p. 231-245) who suggests inter alia (based on Sefer HaChinukh Emor # 313 and Tosafot Shavuot 23b) that the standard may be lower specifically for "shiurim"; and Rav Aryeh Tzvi Frommer (published as Appendix 3 to Sridei Eish 2:4), who argues that "and live by them" extends to significant diminution of vitality short of death.

plainly ill, our fundamental criterion is how they feel. The halakhic challenge is to articulate a standard that either enables a person to determine for themselves whether their subjective experience warrants eating on Yom Kippur, or else enables a posek to evaluate the patient's expression of how they are feeling.

What is the halakhic standard?

Mishnah Yoma 8:5-6 states that an *ubrah* (=pregnant woman) who experiences a food craving on Yom Kippur must be fed "until her *nefesh* is restored", and a person in the throes of a fit (=*bulmus*) must be fed even nonkosher food "until their eyes light up". A Talmudic narrative (Ketubot 61a-b) extends these rules to an ordinary man experiencing a food craving. In all of these cases, the agent of the psak is an outside party, and it seems that he or she is responding based on a visual evaluation of the patient's condition, namely that the *ubrah's nefesh* requires restoration, the eyes of the person in *bulmus* are dimmed, and on Ketubot 61a Rav Ashi saw a *ruach tzora'at* (=leprous spirit) spreading over Mar Zutra. It seems very unlikely that the last condition reflected an imminent danger of death. However, the Mishnah and Talmud provide descriptions of symptoms but no clear standard.

In between the *ubrah* and *bulmus* cases, the Mishnah teaches that in the absence of experts, a *choleh* (= ill person) must be fed on their own authority "until they say 'Enough!'". That is to say, the Mishnah gives an endpoint. What does the patient have to say in order to initiate feeding?

The ROSH and Rabbeinu Tam each report a Talmudic manuscript of Yoma 83a which apparently requires the *choleh* or experts to declare that not feeding the *choleh* carries a risk of death. Each then insists that the text must be either rejected or reinterpreted, on different but compatible grounds. ROSH declares that experts rarely make such a claim directly, while Rabbeinu Tam protests that *choleh*s are not prophets. The upshot of their position, which is adopted by Shulchan Arukh and to my knowledge undisputed in contemporary halakhah, is that the proper standard is "lest the illness intensify and put the *choleh* at risk".

We must ask: "At risk" of what, if not of death? And how does this standard relate to the cases of *ubrah*, *bulmus*, and *ruach tzora'at*?

The best explanation is that *halakhah* recognizes that conditions which are not fatal in themselves may stress a person physically to the point that their constitution is damaged. This may cause either a short-term vulnerability to fatal illnesses etc., or else a long-term weakening that is likely to yield a shortened lifespan. I have confirmed with doctors that this concern still seems reasonable to contemporary medicine. Moreover, they agreed that long COVID is just the kind of condition likely to be a dangerous overall stressor in some cases.

The correct procedure for a person with Long Covid, therefore, is to ask them whether their past experience leads them to believe that fasting will risk causing that sort of intense short-term or sustained weakening. If it will, the second question is whether in their experience this risk can be prevented by eating as soon as certain cues are experienced, or whether such cues come too late or unreliably.

If they believe that fasting risks causing that sort of damage, and that they cannot reliably prevent the risk by drinking or eating on cue, then of course they must not even try to fast. If they believe that eating or drinking on cue is reliably effective, then they may wait to eat until they experience the cues.

The remaining question is what they should eat or drink, and in what amounts.

If they are fully convinced that eating or drinking "shiurim" will suffice, or that they will realize with enough advance notice when "shiurim" are insufficient, then they should begin with "shiurim". However, they should not take risks in this regard, any more than they should with regard to fasting completely.

If sufficient, they should drink only water[10].

If they are certain that this will not prevent them from drinking enough, they may try to 'flavor' the water with something that is not

---

[10] This is because Halakhot Ketanot 2:282 states that drinking water is not Biblically forbidden on Yom Kippur.

food and that almost no one would consume voluntarily except for medicinal purposes. But this is not necessary.

If they need more water than would be possible via the standard practice of "shiurim", they should still drink in amounts of "shiurim" per drink, even if they will need to take many drinks in rapid succession[11].

In principle, there is no need to involve a posek in these evaluations. However, for generally admirable reasons, many people will be too *machmir* on Yom Kippur, and too *meikil* on *pikuach nefesh*, if they take the entire responsibility on themselves. Also, I recognize that there are many conditions other than Long COVID that might be subject to the same psak. Therefore, *cholim* are welcome to contact me at moderntorahleadership@gmail.com to set up times to discuss their specific cases[12].

---

[11] This is because "shiurim" are defined as amount/time, but the baseline halakhah likely has a minimal time for drinking, even though standard practice is to give eating and drinking the same length of time.

[12] Rabbeinu Manoach to Rambam Shevitat Asor 2:9 expresses concern that people may tailor their symptoms to generate a leniency from a posek. However, it seems to me that he refers only to societies where eating on Yom Kippur carries a social cost. In a voluntary society, as confirmed by my experience, the risk of risky *chumra* is much greater than that of unjustified *kula*.

PART V

HALAKHIC ILLUSTRATIONS

Is it coherent to prohibit visual images of invisible things?

Chapter 20

WHAT DO ANGELS LOOK LIKE?
AND
OTHER QUESTIONS ABOUT HALAKHAH's UNDERSTANDING OF ART

"How many angels can dance on a needle's point?" is often seen as a paradigmatically pointless speculation. Wikipedia reports an academic consensus that the question was invented to needle certain schools of philosophy or theology, with Peter Harrison suggesting that "needle's point" was a pun on "needless point". But the underlying issue was and remains serious: Do metaphysical beings occupy physical space?

"What do angels look like?" may seem similarly silly. But Rosh HaShannah 24b provides two possible Biblical sources for a prohibition against producing representations of angels. Shemot 20:4 (also Devarim 5:8) bans the making of representations of things "*in the heavens above*", and Shemot 20:20 bans the making of gold and silver representations of things "*with Me*". If we don't know what angels look like, how can we know whether a particular representation is forbidden?

One possible answer is that they look like *keruvim*, the winged figures atop the Ark. But this answer seems paradoxical, as G-d commanded us to make the *keruvim*! This can be finessed by asserting that the prohibitions prohibit making **additional** images of angels. But that seems forced, and also 1 Kings 6:23 reports that King Shlomoh made two additional wooden *keruvim* for the Temple.

A second possibility is that angels look as described in the visions of Yechezkel, with multiple pairs of wings. But this also seems strange, as before Yechezkel, what did the prohibition mean? Also, do all angels look alike? Yechezkel himself seems to suggest otherwise.

The possibility that seems most compelling to me emerges from Ralbag's Commentary:

 וראוי שתדע
כי צורת האדם - לא יעברו על עשייתה
אם לא היתה בולטת,
כי אינה תמונת האדם
לפי מה שיורגש ממנו בזולת זה האופן,
וזה מבואר בנפשו;
ואולם צורת כוכבים ומזלות –
הנה יעברו עליה
אף על פי שהיא שטוחה,
כי צורתם היא שטוחה לפי מחשבת האנשים.
וכן צורת מלאכי השרת <u>אשר יסכימו האנשים בהם –</u>
יעברו על עשייתה אף על פי שהיא שטוחה,
לפי שאין להם צורות ותמונות על דרך האמת.

You should know
that representations of human beings –
one does not violate by making them
unless they stick up three-dimensionally,
because only in that manner are they *temunot* of a human being
as perceived by human beings,
as is self-explanatory;
but representations of stars and planets/constellations –
one violates (by making them)
even if they are flat (=two-dimensional),
because their actual form is flat according to the way people think;
so too, a representation of ministering angels that people agree on –
one violates by making them even if the representation is flat,
because they (angels) have no forms or images in the way of truth.

Ralbag contends that since angels actually don't look like anything, the prohibition must refer to whatever a particular society recognizes as a visual representation of an angel.

This understanding parallels Rambam's explanation in his Commentary to the Mishnah that prohibitions against representations of the sun, moon, and stars do not relate to the astronomical bodies as they appear to the human eye, but rather to zodiac-like images, whose relationships to the astronomical bodies are entirely products of the human imagination.

The question then is why such representations should be forbidden. A reasonable first step toward answering is to note that the prohibition against representing G-d seems also to be related to His not having "any form or image in the way of truth". Devarim 4:15-16 warns:

וְנִשְׁמַרְתֶּם מְאֹד לְנַפְשֹׁתֵיכֶם
כִּי לֹא רְאִיתֶם כָּל־תְּמוּנָה
בְּיוֹם דִּבֶּר יְקֹוָק אֲלֵיכֶם בְּחֹרֵב
מִתּוֹךְ הָאֵשׁ:
פֶּן־תַּשְׁחִתוּן
וַעֲשִׂיתֶם לָכֶם פֶּסֶל תְּמוּנַת כָּל־סָמֶל
תַּבְנִית זָכָר אוֹ נְקֵבָה . . .

You must be exceedingly guarded for your souls
because you saw no temunah
on the day that Hashem spoke to you at Chorev
from the midst of the fire.
Lest you destroy
and make for yourselves a pesel, a temunah of any semel
a tavnit of a male or a female . . .

The simplest reading of the argument in these verses is that representations are forbidden because they entrench false ideas of G-d in human minds. Recall that *avodah zarah* originally meant "strange worship of G-d" rather than "worship of a strange god".

However, Devarim 4:19 seems to convey a different rationale.

וּפֶן־תִּשָּׂא עֵינֶיךָ הַשָּׁמַיְמָה
וְרָאִיתָ אֶת־הַשֶּׁמֶשׁ וְאֶת־הַיָּרֵחַ וְאֶת־הַכּוֹכָבִים כֹּל צְבָא הַשָּׁמַיִם
וְנִדַּחְתָּ וְהִשְׁתַּחֲוִיתָ לָהֶם וַעֲבַדְתָּם . . .

And lest you raise your eyes toward heaven
and see the sun and the moon and the stars, all the host of heaven
and be led astray into sin, and bow to them, and worship them

The suggestion here seems to be that conceiving of G-d as representable will lead to the worship of astronomical bodies. However, the causal chain is not clear.

The question that seems most pressing to me, and that none of these texts address explicitly, is whether the prohibition against physical representations is intended to constrain our thoughts and imaginations, or even our writing. Should making and reporting mental representations of G-d also be forbidden? (I am leaving aside the halakhic questions of whether objects that create representations via optical illusions are forbidden, or images composed of energy, such as light-sculptures.)

The obvious difficulty with any such prohibition is Yechezkel. The magnificent poem An'im Zemirot suggests that we understand the prohibition as discouraging **unauthorized** mental representations of G-d. It therefore provides us with a handy list of Biblical, i.e. authorized descriptions. The problem is that the Torah seems to ban even, or perhaps especially, physical representations of the prophetic descriptions.

Moreover, if mental or verbal representations of G-d angels are discouraged, we may end up with an irony according to Ralbag. If the prohibition accomplishes its purpose, and conversation and thoughts about G-d and angels become utterly aniconic, then there will be no "representations that people agree on". With regard to G-d, it may be that we prohibit even representations that are meaningful only to the artist. But with regard to angels, Ralbag seems clear that only conventional representations are forbidden. Could each artist then freely produce their own representations?

In other words – can we argue that the ultimate purpose of the prohibition is to free us to think and create about angels subjectively without worrying that the results will be taken as objective representations?

Imagine a society in which everyone agrees that a particular image corresponds to the word "angel", but everyone also understands that the image is no more a representation than is the word "angel". Are such images "agreed on" for Ralbag?

If the prohibition is against "making" rather than "having" representations, what if someone makes a representation that resonates with enough other people that it becomes conventional?

Part of what I'm wondering is whether there are images that human beings are hard-wired to recognize as angels, in a way that culture cannot extirpate. Even if the culture professes not to believe in the existence of angels, if we understand the term, we automatically associate it with certain images.

Here's another thought experiment: What if a culture becomes convinced that angels look just like human beings (at least until they earn their wings)?

What about cultures that believe that angels are masters of disguise? So for example: According to Ralbag, "flat" paintings of human beings are permitted, but not of angels. What if I paint a scene of Avraham serving three men while they eat under a tree? What if I paint the scene but don't title it?

Here's the thing. Most of us live in Jewish cultures that are more-or-less post-Maimonidean in the sense that even non-philosophers instinctively agree that neither G-d nor angels "look like" anything in particular. My sense is that we also live in Jewish cultures that instinctively accept virtually every halakhic leniency regarding the production of images, as can be witnessed by the reaction to occasional efforts by halakhists to impose restrictions on kindergarten drawings of sunny days (or to my wife's objection to the representation of G-d as a benevolently personified moon in a popular children's siddur). It seems clear to me that these realities go hand-in-hand, and can best be justified by arguments along the lines of Ralbag above.

It also seems clear to me that such arguments often implicitly contend that all religious images are fundamentally kindergarten art. They do not take the religious representations produced by artists seriously. That does not seem to me sustainable. The unanswered halakhic questions I've raised throughout this essay are intended to at least raise the issue.

Why I tried to swim against the megillah livestream as we approached Purim 2021, the second "COVID Purim".

Chapter 21

THE PRIVATE HISTORY OF A PSAK THAT FAILED

Let's assume that many synagogues in cold climates cannot provide COVID-safe megillah-readings for their entire membership. Let's also assume that we don't want anyone to risk death from cold or COVID in order to hear the megillah, or even Parshat Zakhor (which we can wait for better weather to fulfill).

I began with a strong feeling that our communities should have invested more energy in training leiners, commissioning klafs, and setting up spreadsheets, to ensure much wider access to a live reading from a kosher megillah. The wonderful efforts of Chabad in New Rochelle last year should have been our model.

Based on that feeling, I thought that our communities were responsible to find a way that almost everyone could fulfill their obligations in a way halakhically preferable to listening to a livestream.

Let me explain that further.

I saw two attitudes toward reliance on livestreaming in public pronouncements.

One was celebratory; the pandemic allowed us to realize that our rejection of the internet as a ritual space was old-fashioned and exclusionary. This is true. It is beyond question that more and more of "real life" is online, and that economic, physical, and emotional limitations make entering the physical space of synagogues very difficult for many people, especially those already on the margins of the community.

A second saw reliance on livestreaming as an emergency measure. The pandemic may well be the kind of extreme *sh'at hadchak* that allows halakhah to give credit for actions that wouldn't be minimally acceptable (*bediavad*) in ordinary times[13].

Each of these approaches made me nervous.

The first approach underplays the costs of decentering physical community. It's easy to see the analogy to the Conservative movement's decisions about cars in the face of the movement to suburbia. It's also easy to see many important differences, both in terms of the sociology and especially in terms of the halakhic approaches; there's nothing beyond the bounds of normal halakhic discourse here. Nonetheless, it seemed to me unnecessarily risky.

I was also unhappy treating a second consecutive Purim as that kind of extreme halakhic emergency. But treating it as an ordinary emergency, and yet making reliance on the livestream widespread, would make it much more likely that this reliance would take long-term root in our communities.

Because of these discomforts, and because I thought we could have done more to prepare, I was looking for another way to enable people to fulfill this mitzvah at home.

Deborah Klapper challenged my assumptions in two ways.

First, she argued that my critique of our lack of preparation was overblown. Not much more could have been done; the weather simply made it impossible.

Second, she thought that because many community rabbis had issued psakim, in reliance on major poskim, telling people that they could rely on the livestream this year, it would be wrong and irresponsible for me to make people feel uncomfortable doing so.

Deborah was certainly correct if I had no viable alternative (and likely even if I did). But my dear friend Dov Weinstein emailed me: "If one is stuck at home with no options but listening to the Megillah over zoom, do you think it would be at least a *hiddur* to have the camera show

---

[13] See How Radically Can Halakhah Change in a Sh'at Hadchak? by Taking Responsibility for Torah (anchor.fm) and Halakha in Crisis Mode: Four Models of Adaptation | jewishideas.org.

a closeup of the *klaf,* such that the person at home can "see" the text, and read along for themselves out of a kosher megillah?"

I had not previously thought about how a visual of the scroll might help.

It seems obvious that for those who have a kosher megillah scroll at home, and are comfortable repeating Biblical Hebrew after dictation, the simplest and best solution is a recording made specifically to allow listeners to repeat it word for word while reading their own scroll. Last year a colleague responded to my request by posting a link to such a recording (68 minutes long) from Rabbi Daniel Mann, and I am told that it is available upon request from info@eretzhemdah.org.

Many people don't have access to a scroll. But if a livestream video combined with livestream dictation would work halakhically, they would not need one. I thought this could be the practical alternative I needed.

Deborah challenged this assumption as well. She argued that I radically overestimated people's comfort and competence at repeating the Hebrew of the megillah after dictation, even if they could look at an unvocalized text while doing so. She also argued that not many people would find this a congenial option; and that even those who tried it would probably make mistakes that would prevent them from fulfilling the mitzvah. If they allowed more competent people to correct them, they would be humiliated as well (and probably still make too many mistakes to fulfill their obligation).

That should probably have been enough to stop me. However, Deborah only got involved after I had already written several drafts of an essay arguing for this proposal.

Here was the initial version of my argument.

In Shu"T Yabia Omer (4OC:8:15), Rav Ovadiah Yosef zt"l understands Shu"T Radbaz (3:605) as holding that if a person reads a text silently, then repeats it out loud immediately while looking away, they are nonetheless considered to be **reading from the text**. (This position is necessary for just about any contemporary *keriat haTorah* to be valid, since *baalei keriah* often look just ahead while reading, especially when they transition between columns.)

Rav Ovadiah contends that Radbaz's position is supported by Sefer haEshkol (via Nimmukei Yosef) and Agudah's position that a blind person can receive an Aliyah. He understands them as requiring the blind person to repeat the Torah reading word for word after someone who is reading directly from the scroll. Rav Ovadiah further contends that Beit Yosef (OC 141) cites their position in the context of ROSH's position that the *oleh* must formally be the Torah reader, with the "official" *baal keriah* serving only to prompt the *oleh*. Therefore, Beit Yosef considers the blind *oleh* to be **reading from the text.**

א"ו

שמכיון שהש"ץ רואה וקורא מתוך הכתב,
והסומא קורא אחריו בנחת
בתכ"ד לראייתו של הש"ץ –
שפיר דמי.
אלמא דלא בעינן שהקריאה של העולה לס"ת תהיה
מתוך הכתב **ממש.**

Rather, it must be
that since the *shaliach tzibbur* sees and reads from the written text,
and the blind person reads after him quietly
immediately after the *shaliach tzibbur* sees that text –
this is halakhically fine.
So we see that we do not require the *oleh*'s reading to be
literally from the written text.

Beit Yosef rejects Sefer HaEshkol's position. The contemporary custom to give aliyot to the blind rests primarily on Maharil (brought by RAMO in Shulchan Arukh OC139:3), who rejects ROSH's position that the *oleh* must read. However, Rav Ovadiah suggests that Beit Yosef rejects HaEshkol only with regard to someone who is blind.

וגם הב"י ודעימיה
שחלקו על האשכול וסיעתו
י"ל שמודים בזה,
רק שבסומא,
הואיל ואינו רואה בעצמו הכתב –
אין לסמוך על ראית הש"ץ וקריאתו,
אבל כשרואה הכתב בעצמו –

אפי' קורא התיבה בע"פ ש"ד.
Even Beit Yosef and those with him,
who disagreed with Eshkol and his posse –
we can say that they concede to this,
and it's only that with regard to a blind person,
since he does not himself see the written text,
we cannot rely on the seeing and reading of the *shaliach tzibbur*,
but when the *oleh* sees the written text themselves –
even if the *oleh* reads the word from memory – it is good.

I thought the simplest explanation for this position is that for the sighted, repeating dictation from a scroll is considered reading from that scroll. However, this extension does not apply to people physically incapable of visual reading (and perhaps not to illiterates). On this basis, a person could probably be considered to be **reading from the text of a megillah** if they repeated it word for word after a livestream of someone reading from a kosher megillah.

However, Dov Weinstein correctly pointed out that Rav Ovadiah's language indicates that Beit Yosef ultimately requires not only the possibility of seeing the written text, but also actually seeing it, even If the seeing and reading need not be exactly simultaneous.

One might argue that Beit Yosef's requirement of actual seeing is necessary only to avoid the negative prohibition against reciting Written Torah from memory (which may be evaded nowadays by reading from a printed or projected text), and not for the positive requirement of reading from a text. But that seems elaborate and speculative, and perhaps also insufficient.

Repeating after a livestream reading from a kosher megillah is therefore effective only according to the position that Beit Yosef rejects. Furthermore, I am not convinced that Eshkol and Agudah in fact required the blind *oleh* to repeat from dictation at all; more likely one or both ruled against ROSH and did not require any *oleh* to read for themselves. Accordingly, repeating after a livestream reading seemed unlikely to move the needle far enough halakhically, even if combined with the possibility that one fulfills the obligation simply by listening to the livestream.

However, there is also extensive halakhic literature about whether various forms of indirect "seeing" count as seeing. The conversation generally begins with Shu"T Halakhot Ketanot 1:99 (see also 1:274) about spectacled *baalei keriah*, but the literature covers *kiddush hachodesh, re'iyat negaim, dayyanei chalitzah*, the blessing said when seeing kings, davening in the presence of excrement, and many other topics. The general outcome is that all these forms of seeing are sufficient. The exceptions are where the indirectness introduces a significantly greater possibility of error.

None of these seeings is halakhically vicarious – no one fulfills anyone else's **obligation of seeing**. Any attempt to do that would be subject to the same rules as attempting to fulfill obligations of speech via a livestream.

However, with regard to *keriat megillah*, the mitzvah is not seeing but **reading**, just with a condition that the reading must be from a scroll. What if one repeats dictation from a livestreamed reading while looking at a video livestream of the megillah being read from? That, I thought would very likely fulfill Beit Yosef's requirement that the repeater be looking at the scroll being dictated from.

So even after Deborah's critique, I thought I still had enough to at least launch a trial balloon for such a reading. What I should have realized, however, was that if there were no longer important practical effects, I needed to do much more extensive research before thinking about publishing.

Happily, a wonderful friend and talmid chakham, Rav Yitzchak Roness, pointed me to https://www.hebrewbooks.org/pdfpager.aspx?req=43794&st=&pgnum=287&hilite= , which contains a much better sourced and developed discussion of the issues associated with my argument. So on my father in-law's theory that "No one is useless – you can always be a bad example", I've written the essay you've read.

The Yerushalmi rules that human dignity overrides active violations of Torah prohibitions, while the Bavli apparently adheres to Rav's ruling that one must endure public nakedness rather than wear shatnez.

Chapter 22

CAN YOU TELL ME HOW THIS RISHON READ THE GEMARA?

On Berakhot 19b, Rav Yehuda states in the name of Rav that a person who becomes aware that their clothing contains shaatnez must remove it "even in the marketplace", meaning even at the cost of public humiliation. The rationale provided is that human wants and needs are irrelevant in the face of Divine commands = אין ואין תבונה ואין עצה לנגד ה'.

The Talmud challenges Rav with five Tannaitic rulings in which halakhah is suspended for the sake of human dignity. Each challenge is resolved by distinguishing the cases; human dignity trumps Halakhah Type A, such as the prohibition against shaatnez, but not Halakhah Type B. The result is that Rav's statement remains legally intact but no longer stands for anything philosophically coherent. If human wants and need are irrelevant in the fac e of Divine commands, why does human dignity trump <u>any</u> such commands?

In the Vilna Talmud, Type B areas of Halakhah includes rabbinic decrees, Biblical monetary obligations, and passive violation of Biblical obligations. Other versions add or substitute Biblical obligations that do not apply equally to all Jews, or that result from annullable vows. A reasonable holistic understanding perhaps found in Tosafot is that the sugya is intended as a vector – each time a new issue comes up, the goal is to find a way to distinguish it from Rav's case without disturbing his ruling in his case. The philosophic import may be that G-d chooses to allow human wants and needs to override Divine commands, so that accounting for them becomes the Divine command, but that we are obligated to recognize that this is neither a necessary nor an unlimited concession. After all, halakhah requires us to sacrifice our lives rather than violate certain commandments!

Keeping this balance in mind requires us to maintain Rav's ruling as an Archimedean point, an absolutely fixed position. Nevertheless, it might move.

Mishnah Kil'ayim 9:1 states אין עראי לכלאים, "there is no temporariness with regard to the prohibition against wearing kil'ayim (=shaatnez). The Yerushalmi thereupon reads:

> If he was walking in the marketplace
> and turned out to be wearing shaatnez –
> two Amoraim (dispute):
> one says 'forbidden', and the other says 'permitted'.
> The one who says 'forbidden' –
> it is a Torah matter;
> The one who says permitted –
> along the lines of what R. Zeira said:
> "Great is human dignity
> in that it pushes the DON'T mitzvah aside for a moment."

The 'permitted' position seems to directly contradict Rav!

However, this contradiction is easily resolved. A version of the statement attributed by the Yerushalmi to R. Zeira is cited as an anonymous (presumed) beraita in the Bavli, apparently to challenge Rav. However, the challenge is actually a lead-in to Rav Sh'va's gloss, endorsed by Rav Kehana, that the DON'T in question refers to the prohibition "Do not stray from what they tell you", which is the source of Rabbinic authority. It seems easy to read this gloss into the Yerushalmi and contend that the Amoraim dispute whether the case of the shaatnez discovered in the marketplace refers to Biblically or Rabbinically prohibited shaatnez, but both agree with Rav that one must remove Biblically prohibited shaatnez at once.

However, Yerushalmi Berakhot 3:1 cannot be explained this way.

The first ruling cited in the Bavli to challenge Rav permits a kohen to accompany a mourner returning from a funeral even via a path that involves corpse-tum'ah, which is forbidden to a kohen. The Bavli resolves the challenge by asserting that tum'ah on a road does not refer to an actual grave but rather to a beit hapras, a space from which human remains have been removed but perhaps not fully. A kohen is only Rabbinically forbidden to traverse a *beit hapras*. The Yerushalmi assumes this interpretation but then states that R. Zeira's statement authorizes kohanim to accompany the mourner even when that involves a Biblical violation.

Recall however that some versions of the Talmud, supported by many rishonim, contend that the Bavli also distinguished Biblical obligations that do not apply equally to all Jews from Rav's ruling. The prime example is the prohibition against becoming *tamei* via contact with a corpse, which applies only to kohanim. So we can reconcile Rav with the Yerushalmi by contending that R. Zeira's statement refers to Rabbinic prohibitions **and** to Biblical prohibitions that do not apply equally to all Jews.

This reconciliation exposes an apparent gap in the Bavli. Rav Kehana defends Rav Sh'va for limiting the beraita "Great is human dignity in that it pushes aside a DON'T in the Torah" to *Don't Stray*, and therefore to Rabbinic prohibitions. (*Don't Stray* is also the source of the Sanhedrin's general authority over Biblical halakhah, but in context Rav Sh'va does not mean to imply that one can defy the Sanhedrin for the purpose of sustaining human dignity. Maybe the people in the beit midrash who laughed at him thought that's what he meant?) But if human dignity also trumps some Biblical obligations, Rav Sh'va's interpretation seems unnecessarily narrow. So while the Bavli doesn't say this outright, perhaps by the end of the sugya Rav Sh'va's interpretation is inoperative.

Reading the Bavli this way opens further possibilities. The fourth challenge in the Bavli to Rav is from the ruling that an 'elder' need not trouble to pick up and then return a lost object that is beneath his or her dignity, despite the Biblical prohibition *You must not look away*. The solution is that the case of lost objects can only be generalized to monetary prohibitions, and not as far as Rav's case of shaatnez. The fifth challenge, from the obligation for even a *nazir* and *kohen gadol* to bury someone who dies without relatives, is resolved by distinguishing between passive and active violations. Many commentators note that not picking up a lost object is also a passive violation. This means that the distinction between monetary and ritual obligations is no longer necessary to defend Rav. Perhaps that means it too is inoperative.

At least at first glance, this would be a stringency. The most straightforward understanding of the Talmud is that human dignity overrides **all** monetary prohibitions, whether active or passive. This outcome seems practically implausible, and various methods have been proposed for evading it. But saying that the monetary/ritual distinction has been cast aside may be the simplest.

We can decide instead that reconciling Rav and the Yerushalmi in Berakhot/Nazir is unnecessary. The Yerushalmi believes that human dignity can override even active violations, whereas the Bavli maintains steadfast allegiance to Rav, and the Bavli's allegiance is sufficient to make our own halakhic position immoveable.

Please note that even this extreme reading of the Yerushalmi would not open a free-for-all in which every individual could decide for themselves what violated their dignity, and in which even the slightest violation of human dignity would justify violating even the most severe Biblical prohibitions. What it would do instead is stimulate the development of carefully calibrated and nuanced system. For example, halakhists working from the Bavli have already distinguished between major and minor dignity violations, or between the dignity of many people and that of individuals (this is also supported by some texts of the Yerushalmi), or between temporary and long-term suspension of halakhah (also supported by the Yerushalmi). They have also specified the conditions under which an 'elder' can look away from a lost object, and distinguished between cases where the relevant human dignity cost is accidental or essential to the halakhah. For example, the halakhah sometimes mandates public humiliation as a punishment for sin! All these distinctions and regulations and more would be needed in an alternate halakhic universe based on the Yerushalmi's rejection of Rav.

What doesn't seem possible is to read the Bavli as rejecting Rav. Nonetheless, at least one medieval reader appears to have done so. I'll provide the text as found in the Peirushim uPsakim shel Rabbeinu Avigdor HaTzarfati # 187 and also in the Tosafist anthology Moshav Zekeinim to Vayikra 19:19, with my translation. (Note: There seems to be great uncertainty or even controversy about the identity of the relevant R. Avigdor.)

(וּבֶגֶד כִּלְאַיִם שַׁעַטְנֵז לֹא יַעֲלֶה עָלֶיךָ)

מכאן תנן:

אין ערָאי לכלאים.

ובירושלמי פליגי אמוראי אי דרבנן הוא או דאורייתא

אם אדם הבין בשוק

שהבגד שהוא לבוש יש בו כלאים –

פושטו מיד למ"ד דאורייתא,

ולמ"ד דרבנן - עד שיגיע לביתו.

וי"מ

דכ"ע אית להו דאורייתא,

ומ"מ משום כבוד הבריות דוחה, וימתין עד שיגיע לביתו.

ואי ק"ק

דהא אמרינן דגדול כבוד הבריות שדוחה לא תעשה - ה"מ בשב ואל

תעשה, אבל בקום ועשה – לא!?

וי"ל

דה"מ כבוד המת,

אבל כבוד הבריות דחיים - דוחה ואפילו בקום ועשה

וכן פר"ץ.

"A garment of mixed kinds shaatnez must not go up on you" –

Based on this verse a Mishnah (Kil'ayim 9:2) teaches:

There is no (leniency of) **temporariness regarding** (the wearing of) **kil'ayim.**

And in the Yerushalmi, Amoraim argue whether this (ban on momentary wearing) is Rabbinic or Biblical.

if a person realized while in the marketplace

that the garment they are wearing contains kil'ayim –

they must remove it immediately according to the opinion that it is Biblical,

but according to the opinion that it is Rabbinic – (they may wait) until reaching home.

But some interpret

that all opinions hold that it is deoraita,

but regardless, because of human dignity it is pushed aside, and they may wait until reaching home.

But if you find this (interpretation) a little difficult
because we say that "Great is human dignity in that it pushes aside
a DON'T" –
applies only when in a passive case, but not in an active case?!
One can respond:
That is only true with regard to the dignity of the dead,
but the dignity of living human beings – pushes (Biblical
prohibitions) aside even actively.
So interpreted R.Z.[14]

The "Some interpret", and the mysterious R.Z. quote the Bavli's
final distinction between active and passive, but then claim that it
applies only to the dignity of the dead, not to that of the living. But that
distinction was introduced to explain why human dignity does not
trump halakhah in the case of Rav, who is dealing with the honor of the
living!? In fact, Rav and the Yerushalmi seem to be discussing the same
case, so how can one even imagine reconciling them?! I look forward
very much to your creative explanations.

---

[14] I don't know to whom this refers.

*With great kavod comes great public scrutiny, because people both want
moral heros and resist them.*

Chapter 23

CHILLUL HASHEM

Before every class trip to the great world outside, my Modern Orthodox
Day School teachers warned us "not to make a *chillul Hashem*"
(desecration of G-d's Name) by misbehaving. The Jewish G-d's public
image was inextricably bound up with our own recognizable Jewishness.
Sometimes the teachers were more optimistic and asked us to make a
kiddush Hashem, but "first do no harm" was generally the spirit.

I think we understood what was wanted and why. We knew that
people judged our parents by our behavior. Many or most of us felt
judged as Jews everywhere we went, all the time. This was just a more
concentrated form of being on display. We also knew that most or
maybe all of us would let the family and religious team down on
occasion. But we generally tried hard.

Was this a fair burden to impose on children? Is it really possible for
children to "make a *chillul Hashem*"?

Rambam Sefer Hamitzvot DON'T #63 declares that the prohibition
against *chillul Hashem* can be divided into three parts. Two of them
relate to all Jews in the same way. These universal violations are

1) transgressing a mitzvah in submission to a religiously
motivated thug, and

2) transgressing a mitzvah with no motive other than to spite G-d.

These cases may seem very different from each other – one involves
surrendering out of self-interest, while the whole point of the other is
that it involves no self-interest. The common denominator is that the
thug in the first case has exactly the same motive as the subject in the
second case. G-d's Name is desecrated when His will is flouted
successfully by someone whose only goal is that it be flouted.

Rambam sets out the third category as follows:

והחלק המיוחד הוא
שיעשה האדם ידוע במעלה והטוב
פעולה אחת
תיראה בעיני ההמון שהוא עבירה
ושאין דמיון הפועל ההוא ראוי לנכבד כמוהו לעשות
אף על פי שיהיה הפועל מותר
הנה הוא חלל את השם.
והוא אמרם (יומא פו א)
היכי דמי חלול השם
כגון אנא דשקילנא בשרא מבי טבחא ולא יהיבנא דמי לאלתר
רבי פלוני אמר:
כגון אנא דמסגינא ארבע אמות בלא תורה ובלא תפלין.
The part that depends on the individual is
when a person who is known for elevation and goodness
does an action that appears in the eyes of the masses to be a
transgression
and that an action of that type is not proper for someone as
respected as he is to do
even though that action is halakhically permitted
behold he has desecrated the Name.
This is what is intended by their saying (Yoma 86a)
What is a case of chillul Hashem?
Like me, who takes meat from the butcher and doesn't give him
the money immediately.
Rabbi Ploni said:
Like me, who walks four cubits without Torah and without tefillin.

Rabbi Chaim Heller (footnotes to his Hebrew translation of the Sefer Hamitzvot) contends that Rambam regularly leaves names out of his citations, and that "Rabbi Ploni" is just an instance of such anonymization. However, this seems to be the only time Rambam uses "Rabbi Ploni" that way.

In the Vilna Talmud, the first example is attributed to Rav, and his phrasing is אי שקילנא, if I were to take meat from a butcher without paying immediately. Many manuscripts leave the subjunctive אי out, as does Rambam, so that presumably was Rambam's text. Without the subjective, the text has Rav describing himself as actually taking the meat on credit. Perhaps Rambam thought it would be disrespectful to mention a great rabbi by name when describing him as desecrating the Name. Perhaps that same reason drove a scribe or reciter to insert the subjunctive.

This approach may help explain the very peculiar section of Talmud that follows Rav's statement.

אמר אביי:

לא שנו אלא באתרא דלא תבעי,

אבל באתרא דתבעי - לית לן בה.

אמר רבינא:

ומתא מחסיא אתרא דתבעי הוא.

Abbayay said:

They only taught Rav's statement about a land where the butchers don't dun,

but in a land where the butchers dun – we have nothing against the one who behaves like Rav.

Said Ravina:

And Mata Mechasya is a land where the butchers dun.

The text is very unstable here (the first statement is most likely anonymous rather than by Abbayay, and Rambam almost certainly had a version in which Rav's statement was specifically about a land where butchers do dun) and commentators have struggled to clarify its meaning. Their basic problem is that Rav has to do something very wrong, in order to desecrate the Name, but not too wrong, or else he would be in violation of *lo tonu*, the prohibition against unjustly delaying payment. Anyone who would violate *lo tonu* does not cause a desecration of the Name when they misbehave, since no one identifies them with the Name. The calibration required is very fine.

I suspect there is another basic problem. Is Rav's statement intended as straightforward halakhah, or does it have an element of humor?

On Sotah 49b, a beraita teaches that "once Rebbe was dead, humility and fear of sin ceased to be". But Rav Yosef said to a reciter of that beraita:

לא תיתני ענוה, דאיכא אנא
Do not teach "humility", as there is me!

Oceans of ink have been spilled to explain how Rav Yosef could have made this statement humbly. Benjamin Franklin, by contrast, recognized that the paradox is inescapable. "There is perhaps no one of our natural passions so hard to subdue as pride. Beat it down, stifle it, mortify it as much as one pleases, it is still alive. Even if I could conceive that I had completely overcome it, I should probably be proud of my humility". It seems to me likely that Rav Yosef understood this as well, and that his comment included a significant element of self-satire.

Perhaps there is a line from בגון אנא to דאיכא אנא. If Rambam is correct, the third kind of *chillul Hashem* applies only to renowned scholars. Giving oneself as an example is therefore inherently an act of hubris, and the best way to counteract that is by presenting oneself as actually violating the norm under discussion. "What is an example of *chillul Hashem*? For example, when I . . . "

But subsequent generations could not leave that presentation untouched, lest it be taken literally. So they explained that Rav did not actually desecrate the Name; rather, he acted in a manner that would have desecrated the Name in a society with different expectations. Expectations are always variable, so there was likely an element of ruefulness in Rav's example – perhaps he wished to hold himself to an even higher standard, or worried that his butcher was already doing so. Ravina rushes in to disambiguate further – Mata Mechasya, Rav's hometown (according to the Letter of Rav Sherira Gaon, Mata Mechasya = Sura), was the kind of place where Rav's behavior raised no eyebrows at all.

What about Rabbi Yochanan? He speaks of walking four amot without Torah and tefillin – why would he do that, if that desecrated the Name?

The simplest answer, perhaps found in Rashi, is that Rav Yochanan was old, and no longer capable of maintaining the sort of concentration that people expect of him. He was also not capable of sitting still the entire day. So his reply is a different form of rueful humor – his greatness has led to a situation in which he inevitably desecrates the Name. Publicly proclaiming his frailty might solve that problem. But is that disclosure a cost he should be obligated to bear?

Rambam in Mishneh Torah (Hilkhot Yesodei HaTorah 5:11) provides more detail:

ויש דברים אחרים שהן בכלל חילול השם,
והוא שיעשה אותם אדם גדול בתורה ומפורסם בחסידות
דברים שהבריות מרננים אחריו בשבילם,
ואף על פי שאינן עבירות
הרי זה חילל את השם
כגון שלקח ואינו נותן דמי המקח לאלתר,
והוא שיש לו ונמצאו המוכרים תובעין והוא מקיפן,
או שירבה בשחוק או באכילה ושתיה אצל עמי הארץ וביניהן,
או שדבורו עם הבריות אינו בנחת ואינו מקבלן בסבר פנים יפות אלא בעל
קטטה וכעס,
וכיוצא בדברים האלו
הכל לפי גדלו של חכם
צריך שידקדק על עצמו ויעשה לפנים משורת הדין;

There are other things also within the category of chillul Hashem
namely when a person who is great in Torah and famed for his
chassidut/piety
does things that cause the people to gossip negatively about him,
even though they are not transgressions –
behold he has desecrated the Name.
For example, if he took without paying for his purchase
immediately,
and he has the money, and the sellers are dunning, and he insists
that they give him credit,
or if he spends too much time in play or eating and drinking with
or among ignorami,
or if his speech with the public is not calm
and he receives them not with a pleasant countenance, but
rather is a man of quarrels and anger,
or similar things.
In everything, in proportion to the greatness of the sage,
he must be strict with himself and act beyond the line of the law.

The statement "In everything, in proportion to the greatness of the sage" seems to leave children, and perhaps the rest of us, out of the equation entirely. However, R. Yosef David Azulai ("CHIDA": Shu"T Chayyim Sho'al 2:43) contends that this makes little sense. Whether an action is a chillul Hashem depends on the observer, not the actor. He therefore concludes that

נראה פשוט דה"ה
מי שמוחזק בעירו שהוא גדול
אף כי באמת איננו גדול,
ומכיר הוא בעצמו
מ"מ, כיון דמתחשב הוא אצל ההמון לגדול –
הוא ח"ה.
It seems obvious that the same is true
regarding someone who is reputed in his city to be great
even though he is not actually great,
and recognizes this about himself,
nonetheless, since he is considered by the masses to be great –
he desecrates the Name.

R. Azulai uses this approach to get Rav out of the humility paradox. Rav thought his public reputation undeserved, but could not deny that it existed. Therefore, using himself as an example of chillul Hashem was not arrogant.

I wonder whether there is a transactional element to the way Rambam conceives of this mitzvah. To violate chillul Hashem, you have to be a person held in great public esteem. Whether you deserve the honor, and whether you want it, are irrelevant. With great kavod comes great responsibility. And also – great public scrutiny, because people both want moral heros and resist them.

All of Rambam's examples stay within the Jewish community, though. What are the standards for chillul Hashem outside the community? I think my teachers assumed that all Jews – children, also institutions and states - bear the kind of responsibility outside the community that great sages bear inside it.

The way to avoid that responsibility is to lower expectations. But I think that Rav and Rav Yochanan's humor can do well for us here. With a certain amount of genuine ambivalence, we should aspire to be the kind of people and nation that is capable of making a chillul Hashem.

If "in my humble opinion" marks a claim of originality, how can genuine humility be expressed?

Chapter 24

I HAVE NEVER BEEN WRONG.
(Once, I thought I had erred, but barukh Hashem I was mistaken.)

The Torah's narrative of the eight days during which Aharon and his sons were invested as *kohanim* (the *miluim* period) begins in Parashat Tetzaveh, goes on hiatus until the end of Parashat Tzav, and sort of concludes in Parashat Shemini, with an epilogue in Parashat Acharei Mot. This scattered trail makes it very hard to reconstruct what happened when.

We can say with some confidence that a moral of the story is that *kohanim* have a dangerous job. In Vayikra 8:35, Mosheh tells Aharon and his sons not to leave the entrance to the Ohel Moed for seven days "*and that way you won't die*"; they all survive that period, only for Nadav and Avihu to die on the eighth day. In 10:7, Mosheh warns them not to leave the entrance that day to mourn "*lest you die*". In 10:9, God tells Aharon directly of a prohibition against consuming alcohol before entering Ohel Moed "*and that way you won't die*"; and in 16:2 G-d tells Mosheh to tell Aharon not to come at will into the Kodesh "*and that way he won't die*".

Given the deadly peril awaiting a misstep, it seems only fair for Aharon to have a supremely detailed manual telling him exactly what to do in every circumstance. He should also be able to ask Mosheh for a 'lifeline' whenever a situation not covered by the manual arises.

It's therefore astonishing that Mosheh seems not to have given Aharon instructions about whether to eat sacrifices while in the period called *aninut*, when relatives (such as Nadav and Avihu) have died but are not yet buried. It's even more astonishing that this turns out to be a good thing, because Mosheh Rabbeinu's instructions would have been wrong.

Mosheh expresses impatience/anger/frustration (10:16-18) that one of the *chatat* sacrifices has been burnt rather than eaten. But when Aharon questions whether G-d would have been pleased had he acted differently, Mosheh seems to acknowledge that Aharon acted correctly (10:19-20).

וַיְדַבֵּ֨ר אַהֲרֹ֜ן אֶל־מֹשֶׁ֗ה
הֵ֣ן הַיּ֞וֹם הִקְרִ֣יבוּ אֶת־חַטָּאתָ֣ם וְאֶת־עֹלָתָם֮ לִפְנֵ֣י יְקֹוָק֒
וַתִּקְרֶ֥אנָה אֹתִ֖י כָּאֵ֑לֶּה
וְאָכַ֤לְתִּי חַטָּאת֙ הַיּ֔וֹם
הַיִּיטַ֖ב בְּעֵינֵ֥י יְקֹוָֽק׃
וַיִּשְׁמַ֣ע מֹשֶׁ֔ה
וַיִּיטַ֖ב בְּעֵינָֽיו׃

Aharon spoke to Mosheh:
Yea, today they have sacrificed their *chatat*-sacrifice and their
wholly-burnt sacrifice before Hashem
and these things happened to me
Had I eaten *chatat* today
would that have been good in Hashem's eyes?
Mosheh heard
and it was good in his eyes.

How did Aharon reach his conclusion? Chazal reconstruct a sophisticated halakhic rationale. A *kohen* in *aninut* is generally forbidden to eat sacrifices. However, Mosheh had instituted a special decree (*hora'at sha'ah*) mandating them to eat the *minchah*. Did that decree apply as well to the relevant *chatat*? It turns out that three different *chatats* were brought, two of them for the special circumstance of the *miluim*, and one because the day was *Rosh Chodesh*. Aharon understood that the special decree permitting eating sacrifices while in *aninut* applied only to the special-circumstance *chatats*, whereas Mosheh mistakenly thought that the decree applied throughout.

This reconstruction plainly assumes many details that are not explicit in the text. Even granting them all, a new problem arises. In 10:12-15, Mosheh instructs Aharon, along with Elazar and Itamar "his remaining sons", to eat the leftovers of the *minchah* offering as well as the *shok haterumah* and *chazeih hatenufah* from the *zivchei shelamim*. Why didn't he give instructions regarding the *chatat* at the same time? The simplest explanation is that it was burnt before he arrived, but a *beraita* on Yoma 5b, as explained by all rishonim I have seen, takes a different approach.

כִּי כֵן צֻוֵּיתִי, כַּאֲשֶׁר צִוִּיתִי, כַּאֲשֶׁר צִוָּה ה':
כִּי כֵן צֻוֵּיתִי - בַּאֲנִינוּת יֹאכְלוּהָ;
כַּאֲשֶׁר צִוִּיתִי - בִּשְׁעַת מַעֲשֶׂה אָמַר לָהֶם;
כַּאֲשֶׁר צִוָּה ה' - וְלֹא מֵאֵלַי אֲנִי אוֹמֵר.

(Scripture in this unit of narrative contains three phrases of command:)
"Because I have been commanded so", "as I have commanded", "as Hashem commanded":
"Because I have been commanded so" – that they must eat it (=*the minchah*) even while in *aninut*;
"as I have commanded" – this is what Mosheh said to them when it happened;
"as Hashem commanded" – and I do not say this of my own (authority)

Tosafot HoRosh presents the consensus interpretation:

"וְלֹא מֵאֵלַי אֲנִי אוֹמֵר" –
כְּלוֹמַר: אַל תִּהְיוּ סְבוּרִים שֶׁכְּמוֹ שֶׁטָּעִיתִי בִּשְׂעִיר שֶׁל ר"ח,
כָּךְ אֲנִי טוֹעֶה בֶּחָזֶה וָשׁוֹק,
דְּוַדַּאי צִוָּה הַקָּדוֹשׁ בָּרוּךְ הוּא כָּךְ, וְלֹא מֵאֵלַי אֲנִי אוֹמֵר.
אַף עַל גַּב דְּסֵדֶר הַפְּסוּקִים אֵינוֹ כָּךְ - אֵין מֻקְדָּם וּמְאֻחָר בַּתּוֹרָה.

"and I do not say this to you on my own (authority)":
Meaning: Don't think that just as I erred about (eating) the goat of the Rosh Chodesh sacrifice,
so too I am erring about the *chazeh* and *shok* (of the *zivchei shelamim*)
because the Holy Blessed One **definitely** commanded this, and I do not say this of my own (authority).
Even though the order of the verses is not this way -
there is no 'before' and 'after' in the Torah (= its narratives are not chronologically ordered).

The "order of the verses is not this way" because "as Hashem commanded" occurs in the text <u>before</u> Mosheh errs about the Rosh

Chodesh goat. Yet the consensus interpretation reads Mosheh's
emphasis on this being Hashem's command as a response to Aharon
and his sons losing confidence in him <u>because of</u> that error. It's unclear
why they would respond well to this assurance. If he was mistaken last
time about what G-d intended, why not again?

Perhaps because of this problem, Netziv in <u>Haamek Davar</u>
reinterprets against all the rishonim. He notes that in Vayikra 7:30, the
Torah speaks of waving the *chazeh* but not the *shok*, but that in 9:21,
Aharon waves the <u>chazot and shok "as Mosheh commanded"</u>. In 10:15,
Aharon waves both *shok* and *chazeh*, and actually doesn't mention
eating at all. Netziv concludes that 9:21 describes Aharon as obeying
Mosheh because waving the *shok* was then a *hora'at sha'ah*, a
suspension of ordinary Torah law. 10:15 made waving the *shok* ordinary
halakhah, "as Hashem commanded".

ונראה דהא דאי' ביומא ד"ה ב' ע"ז המקרא "ולא מאלי אני אומר" –
קאי אתנופת השוק,
ולא כפרש"י שם
שפי' הכל לענין אכילה באנינות,
שהרי לא מיירי בזה המקרא באכילה כלל:
It seems that when Yoma 5b says regarding this verse "and I am not
saying this on my own authority" –
it refers to the waving of the *shok*,
as against Rashi's commentary there
which explains all (three phrases of command) as referring to eating
while in *aninut*,
because this verse is not talking about eating at all.

However, Netziv is more cautious in his Talmud commentary
<u>Meromei Sadeh</u>.

ולולא פירש"י
הייתי אומר דקאי
על הא דצוה להניף את החזה יחד עם שוק הימין
If it were not for Rashi's commentary,
I **would** have said that this (= "as Hashem commanded") refers
to the command to wave both the *chazeh* and *shok*

A search of the Bar Ilan Responsa database reveals that Netziv uses the subjunctive לולא = "If it were not for" this way more than seventy times in Meromei Sadeh; five times in his responsa collection Meishiv Davar; once in the extended notes section of his Torah commentary, called Harchev Davar; and **never** in Haamek Davar. So it seems to me that the difference here reflects something beyond this specific case.

What does "If it were not for" really mean?

A draft article I submitted as a teenager to the RIETS journal Beit Yitzchak contained many iterations of *nir'eh laaniyut da'ati*, "it seems to my impoverished intellect". The editors made me remove them on the ground that "you don't actually have that many *chiddushim* (creative points)". I learned that "it seems to my impoverished intellect" marks a claim of originality, and "if it were not for" marks a claim of great originality.

But this cynical approach can't be correct here. Aside from Netziv's character, it can't account for why the same reading is introduced by "were it not" in one of Netziv's books and not another.

A more likely explanation relates to genre. Netziv sees a need to gesture toward authority when the when the field is Talmud commentary, but not when engaging in Bible commentary.

Maybe that's because Netziv thinks Talmud commentary is generally a fit source for halakhic decisionmaking, whereas Torah commentary is not. (This would explain the uses in Meishiv Davar as well as the use in Harchev Davar, which is often more about Talmud than Torah). A claim that one's creative interpretation is better than the one sanctified by tradition is more destabilizing in the realm of Talmud than in Torah, because a long tradition holds that legal interpretation of Torah is a world unto itself that can ignore or uproot what might be the best literary reading.

If it were not for my predecessors, I would suggest the following. Neither Mosheh nor Aharon was necessarily correct about whether Aharon should have eaten the *chatat*. However, Mosheh had a presumptive interpretation, that it should be eaten. He therefore was upset to find that Aharon had burnt it. But when Aharon offered a reasonable interpretation to justify his behavior, Mosheh's reaction was not to overrule him, but rather to say happily "My brother has defeated me, My brother has defeated me".

Had Mosheh insisted on his own interpretation, he would have won the battle, but lost the war. The point was not to establish his personal authority, which would not outlive him, but rather the authority of Revelation. Mosheh's demonstration of humility and integrity, his recognition that his own interpretation was not the same thing as G-d's Word, established him as utterly trustworthy when he claimed Revelation directly, and thus established the authority of Revelation forever.

It is often tempting to overplay the relationship between technological and halakhic changes.

Chapter 25

DEFINING "DYING"

Wallace Stevens wrote that poetry results from "the pressure of reality on the imagination". Similarly, practical halakhah results from the pressure of reality on Torah. The practice of halakhah inevitably changes when reality does. But the **way** in which it changes is often badly misunderstood.

Let's use the halakhic category "*goses*" (roughly: "dying person") as an illustration. Specifically, I want to examine my teacher Rabbi J. David Bleich's contention in Tradition 30:3 that "It appears that any patient who may reasonably be deemed capable of potential survival for a period of seventy two hours cannot be considered a *goses*".

Medical prognosis is affected by medical technology. Under Rabbi Bleich's definition, many conditions categorized as *goses* in past centuries would not be *goses* nowadays, for example because mechanical ventilation might extend their lives. So the practical halakhah of *goses* might change in response to technological change. By contrast, if we adopted a definition of *goses* based purely on symptoms, halakhah on this issue might be static.

Please recognize that neither approach makes today's halakhah dependent on yesterday's science. Neither suggested definition of *goses* binds us to what past medical or halakhic authorities determined to be the life-expectancy of patients with specific medical conditions.

The Talmud asks two basic questions about the *goses*.

The first is one of definition: Is the *goses* alive? The answer to that question is an unequivocal yes. For example, a *goses* can issue a bill of divorce, and killing a *goses* is capital murder. The geonic *Masekhet Semakhot* formulates the rule clearly: "The *goses* is treated the same as a living person for all matters".

The second question is about probability: Is the *goses* **still** alive? Ordinary people have a *chezkat chayyim*, a presumption of continued life. Therefore, for example, a husband's agent may deliver a bill of divorce to a wife without checking whether the husband is still alive, and thereby free her from the obligation of *yibum*. What if the husband was a *goses* at the time of appointment? Rava is cited on Gittin 28a as saying that because "Most *gosesin* progress to death", one cannot deliver a divorce from a *goses*, but his position is refuted by Abbayay. Shavuot 37b and Arakhin 18a cite "Most *gosesin* etc." as the position rejected by an authoritative text. The result again is that status as a *goses* has no legal implications. The known *goses* is alive, and the unknown *goses* is presumptively alive.

Geonic halakhah introduces a new issue. Does the condition of *goses* introduce additional stringencies because of life's fragility? The answer in Masekhet Semakhot (1:1-6) is yes. Actions that are perfectly permissible with regard to healthy people are prohibited as possible murder with regard to a *goses*.

The sixteenth century work Shiltei Gibborim, citing the 13th century Sefer Chasidim, suggests a radical fourth question. Is there an obligation to keep a *goses* alive? Shiltei Gibborim is cited by Rav Mosheh Isserles in Darkei Mosheh and then in his HaMappah supplement to Rav Yosef Caro's Shulchan Arukh,

The answer based on the Talmud and geonim should be "yes", since "The *goses* is treated the same as a living person for all matters". Nonetheless, many authorities understand Rabbi Isserles as saying that the answer is "no". For the purposes of this article only, I will assume the position of those authorities. According to this position, one may withhold life-extending treatment from a *goses*.[15] None of these discussions offers an explicit definition or description of "*goses*".

The great 13th century posek R. Meir of Rothenburg (MAHARAM) may provide one data point. In a responsum that exists in several variants, he orders a woman to begin mourning her husband on the basis of witnesses to the husband having been *goses* at least three days

---

[15] Please see
http://www.torahleadership.org/categories/angelendlife8_21_4_1_.pdf for my own understanding of Rav Isserles.

earlier. (Some understand: "on the basis of witnesses that he had already been *goses* for three days". But this is very difficult to square with MAHARAM's language.) In other words, MAHARAM allowed and required the woman to assume her husband's death at least for the purposes of mourning.

MAHARAM's ruling is apparently endorsed by R. Caro in Shulchan Arukh YD 339:2, and R. Isserles appends the gloss "because he has certainly died already".

The second edition of the 17th century Beit Shmuel (to Shulchan Arukh Even HaEzer 17, n. 94) seems to understand MAHARAM as allowing the woman to remarry on the basis of the same testimony. This leniency has been widely criticized and rejected by subsequent authorities such as Shaagat Aryeh and Noda b'Yehudah.

Beit Shmuel's critics ask an apparently devastating question. We have seen that the Talmud rejects using "Most *gosesin* (progess) to death" as a legal source!? MAHARAM's ruling must therefore apply only to mourning, which is a special case in Halakhah because "the law follows the lenient position with regard to mourning". (Tosafot to Yebamot 120b cites an unknown Tannaitic text, perhaps a variant of one found in the Talmud, as explicitly stating "One does not testify regarding someone who was *goses* that he is dead and his wife may remarry". But MAHARAM may not have had access to t that variant, or may have rejected it.)

Beit Shmuel's defenders respond that Rav Isserles in his gloss to Shulchan Arukh Even HaEzer 17:5 rules that a woman is forbidden to mourn a husband's death on the basis of evidence insufficient to allow her remarriage. It follows that by endorsing MAHARAM's permission to mourn, Rav Isserles was permitting her to remarry.

Beit Shmuel's critics respond that R. Caro's formulation endorsed by Rav Isserles in YD 339:2 does not say husband, but rather "relative" – perhaps it does not include wives. They note that Tur YD 339 cites MAHARAM with regard to "a father or brother" rather than a husband.

Defenders respond that Beit Yosef cites MAHARAM from other sources that in all extant versions refer to a wife, and that even his citation of Tur leaves out the reference to "father and brother".

In my humble opinion, while there is room to discuss Rav Caro's position, Beit Shmuel is almost certainly the correct explanation of Rav Isserles. My evidence is that in his commentary Darkei Mosheh to Tur YD 339's citation of MAHARAM, Rav Isserles cites Shiltei Gibborim's position that there is no obligation to keep a goses alive. This proves that he saw MAHARAM's position as extending well beyond the realm of mourning. Coupled with his use of the term "*vadai*", this seems to me conclusive evidence that Beit Shmuel understood him correctly.

We must still explain how this understanding of Maharam fits with the Talmud's rejection of "Most *gosesin* (progress) to death" as a legal source.

The simplest explanation is that the Talmud's rejection applies only to periods shorter than three days. This is supported by Rav Isserles' comment that "he has **certainly** died by then", which seems intended to distinguish this case from the "**Most** *gosesin*" rule.

It is vital to understand that even Rav Isserles does not mean by **certainly** that there are no exceptions. "Certainly", *vadai*, is a legal term of art; it means that the exceptions are rare enough that the law does not need to account for them. Beit Shmuel contends that this legal certainty is sufficient not only to mandate mourning, but also to permit remarriage.

On what basis did MAHARAM, as understood by Beit Shmuel, limit the Talmud's rejection of "Most *gosesin* (progress) to death" to periods shorter than three days, and assert legal certainty of death for periods longer than that?

I see two basic possibilities.

The first is that MAHARAM had a clear and sufficient medical definition of *goses*. He then determined that in his time and place, such *gosesin* died within three days at a rate sufficient to create legal certainty.

The second possibility is that MAHARAM had a clear and sufficient legal definition of *goses*. One element of that definition was that the person must be legally certain to die within three days.

Either way, the halakhah in MAHARAM's case would change if the availability of ventilation changed a person's prognosis. Suppose for example that witnesses reported nowadays that a husband had the exact same condition as was reported to MAHARAM, but that medical technology had improved to the point that one could not be legally certain of death until after seven days. According to the first possibility, the wife could not begin mourning until the eighth day, because that was now the law for a *goses*. According to the second possibility, the wife could not begin mourning even on the eighth day, because her husband is no longer considered to have been a *goses*.

However, the halakhah in Shiltei Gibborim's case would change only according to the second possibility. Shiltei Gibborim is the only case I can think of where the legal category *goses* affects the law directly, rather than serving as a proxy for a claim about medical prognosis. According to the first possibility, it would be permitted to withhold life-extending treatment from the husband; according to the second, it would not be.

Rabbi Bleich adopts the second possibility. Thus "It appears that any patient who may reasonably be deemed capable of potential survival for a period of seventy two hours cannot be considered a *goses*".

Which possibility is more likely correct? We can't know what MAHARAM thought, because his case comes out the same either way; and we can't know what Shiltei Gibborim thought, because he does not mention a specific time limit. However, I think Rabbi Isserles held the second possibility. Here's why.

MAHARAM's case applies the *goses* category post facto – three days later, one can assume the husband is dead. Shiltei Gibborim (according to the position we are assuming) applies it prospectively – one can withhold treatment from someone the moment they become a *goses*. If so, why does Rav Isserles cite it with regard to MAHARAM, who adds nothing but the time limit? The most likely answer is that the time limit is part of the definition, and one can only withhold treatment now from someone who will with legal certainty die within three days.

One can accept this argument while rejecting Beit Shmuel's position allowing remarriage. Many authorities have explained that remarriage is subject to uniquely high standards of certainty, especially ab initio. So there is no reason to assume that Noda b'Yehudah and Shaagat Aryeh etc. disagree with Rav Isserles' definition of *goses*.

Reality can put other relevant pressures on halakhah. We might for instance argue that medical progress has created a new class of people regarding whom it is ethical not to provide life-extending treatment, **even though** they do not fit the category of *goses* as defined by our precedents. Or we might argue that MAHARAM defined *goses* by **quality-of-life-expectancy**, so that the possibility of prolonging unconscious life on a ventilator would not affect MAHARAM's definition, even though it would have affected his ruling about remarriage. But we must acknowledge that rejecting these arguments does not entail ignoring reality or precedent.

It is tempting to assume that poskim who reach results we dislike on issues of technological change must be ignoring the science or distorting the sources. The truth is that sometimes they are expressing very in-the moment moral opinions that disagree with ours.

I pray that this essay helps spur a return to halakhic tradition.

Chapter 26

A REPENTANT DAYYAN EXPLAINS HOW A STANDARD BEIT DIN PROCESS OPPRESSES CONVERTS

Dear Rabbi Klapper,

I am an Orthodox convert who recently went through an exceedingly bitter divorce. My husband Shimshon became abusive shortly after our marriage, and he used his superior Torah knowledge as a means of controlling me. It took me a long time to realize this. I'm trying very hard to stop seeing halakhah that way, but for now, while I still believe in Torah intellectually, and I'm completely committed to being Jewish, I'm not emotionally able to follow the laws of Shabbes and kashrus punctiliously. I hope to do so again when I've healed.

Thank G-d, at the start of negotiations our lawyers insisted that we sign the Boston Agunah Task Force agreement binding us to complete our halakhic divorce before finalizing a settlement. So I didn't have to fight Shimshon for the *get* (halakhic bill of divorce).

When we came to beit din, though, I was very hurt and surprised when the rabbis asked me questions about my observance. I asked them why, and after a series of evasions, they replied that my husband had said that I no longer kept Shabbes, and if so, they needed to write my name in the get as *hagiyores* rather than as *bas Avrohom Avinu*.

This was shocking and deeply hurtful to me. I felt like my adopted family was abandoning me in my time of need. Worse, it felt like they were siding with my abuser. Did Avrohom Avinu, embodiment of chesed, really not want his name associated with mine?! What about all the times that rabbis had assured me that "convert" was a compliment, not a term of derision? What about all the laws against oppressing converts?

I was honest, and they wrote "hagiyores", and I took the get – I felt that I had no choice. I have a friend who walked away from the get process after a similar experience, and is now remarried without a get, with a child at risk of being declared a *mamzer*.

My question to you is – do all batei din do this, or were I and my friend just unlucky? It seems strange to me for halakhah to be so cruel to converts when they are so vulnerable, and to judge them so absolutely at a point that is obviously transitional. Is that what Hashem wants?

Sincerely,

Timna A. (Note: Timna A. is a fictionalized composite portrait.)

Dear Timna,

I'm deeply sorry and profoundly embarrassed to hear your story. Yes, to the best of my knowledge that's what all American batei din do. Yes, this practice is an obvious violation of the Torah's many prohibitions against causing psychological distress to converts (ona'at hager). No, it is not halakhically necessary or even desirable.

But there is an even worse underlying truth. Israeli batei din may take the absence of "ben/bat Avraham Avinu" in a convert's get as a basis for challenging the validity of the conversion, even after several generations.

I write as a penance/maaseh teshuvah for having participated as a dayyan in this recently developed practice. I pray that this response to you, and the more comprehensive as-yet-unpublished article it is drawn from, will help generate a rapid return to tradition.

American batei din today conventionally distinguish two classes of converts when they write a get. Converts who are halakhically observant at the time of divorce are identified as "ben/bat Avraham Avinu". Those who aren't halakhically observant at the time of divorce are identified as "hager/hagiyoret", with no father's name.

This is intrinsically problematic – there is no reason for batei din to judge the observance level of anyone appearing before them for divorce (and batei din generally claim that they don't). It is also technically problematic: for example, the investigation is necessarily cursory and relies on a halakhically inadmissible confession (ayn adam oseh atzmo rasha) and/or testimony from an interested party (nogeia badavar). But the worst part is that some Israeli rabbinic courts and agencies may take the absence of "ben/bat Avraham Avinu" in a convert's get as a basis for challenging the conversion, sometimes even several generations down the line.

This is made explicit by Dayyan Mordekhai Ralbag in Avnei Mishpat 4:13:

"If the divorcing man or women are converts who observe the mitzvot
one should write *ben/bat Avraham Avinu.*
But if they do not observe mitzvot,
**and there is a concern that at the time of conversion they did not
intend to accept the yoke of the commandments and the
conversion is not good and they are Gentiles –**
one must hint at this in the get,
and therefore one should write only their names and conclude with
"*haGer/haGiyoret*".

Dayyan Ralbag's rule makes the presence of *haGer/haGiyoret* in a get a clear basis for challenging the presumed validity of a conversion[16]. (Dayyan Ralbag was recently appointed by his brother in-law, Chief Rabbi Dovid Lau, to head the beit din system in Yerushalayim. The appointment is on hold because the Attorney General has charged that the process was nepotistic, but Rabbi Ralbag is certainly an intellectually impressive and influential dayyan).

Dayyan Ralbag was cited to just that end by Rabbi Shimon Yakobi in his 2010 bookביטול גיור עקב חוסר כנות בקבלת המצוות (Nullification of Conversion Owing to Lack of Sincerity When Accepting the Mitzvot).

Rabbi Yakobi argued that beit din records showing that the majority of Israeli gittin used "*hager/giyoret*" rather than "*ben/bat Avraham Avinu*" supported the decision by Rabbi Avraham Sherman of the Beit Din HaGadol to retroactively invalidate en masse thousands of

---

[16] Dayan Ralbag presents this rule as recording the practice of the Beit Din of Rav Shlomo Fisher. It is possible that Rabbi Fisher limited the use of hager/hagiyoret to cases where the conversion was questionable for reasons additional to the convert's present lack of full observance. However, in practice *batei din* make no investigation beyond asking the parties about their level of observance. (I thank Yael Klausner for raising this point.)

Rabbinate-authorized conversions (Rabbi Yakobi's statistical argument was compellingly refuted by Rabbi David Bass and Rabbi Mordekhai Brully, as cited by Rabbi Yisroel Rozen, אוהב גר, p. 217. Rabbi Sherman's own grounds are beyond the scope of this article. Regardless, his decision served notice that he and his supporters would not refrain from challenging Orthodox conversions even many years later. In other words, it put all converts in permanent fear of challenges to their own or their descendants' Jewishness. I can attest that it had this effect based on contemporary phone calls to the Boston Beit Din and many conversations in subsequent years. Sometimes the ends justify the means; but it would take ultimately important ends to justify such an enormous violation of ona'at hager.)

There is no historical precedent for the procedure Rabbi Ralbag records. The closest model is the late 18th century Toras Gittin (129:11), who insisted that one ought not write ben/bat Avraham Avinu for converts who subsequently apostasized, in other words who explicitly denied their connection to and membership in the Jewish people. The Tel Aviv beit din seems to have extended it to public Sabbath desecrators in the 1950s, and then at some later point to all converts who admitted not being shomrei Shabbat. But no one argued that this practice was halakhically necessary, and empirical evidence shows that it is still not standard in Israel. However, Rabbi Yaakobi reports that it nonetheless became the recommended practice in several manuals of beit din practice.

I found two cases prior to Rav Yaakobi of dayyanim trying to use the language of the get as evidence. The first, from 1972, cited a 1950s Tel Aviv get's use of hager to support a claim that an alleged convert had never stopped being Christian and in fact had never appeared before a beit din. This argument was intended to prevent children born to the (deceased) convert's wife and another man before the get from being classified as mamzerim. The second cited a 1970s Tel Aviv get's use of bat Avraham Avinu as evidence that the convert must at least have claimed to be shomeret Shabbat. This was intended to enable the convert's granddaughter to be classified as Jewish. Neither case made a claim that went beyond the Toras Gittin, and neither made a claim about practice outside of Tel Aviv.

It seems that the Tel Aviv expansion of Toras Gittin reached these shores quite recently. Rav Gedaliah Felder's mid-20th century Nachalat Tzvi cites even Toras Gittin's position as "there are those who say", with a note that it applies only *lekhatchilah*. Similarly, Rabbi Ephraim Eliezer Yulis (Divrei Efraim Eliezer EH 219), Av Beit Din of Philadelphia, responded to a report of the first case above by noting that decisors throughout the ages had made clear that "*hager*" and "*ben Avraham Avinu*" were both valid for all male converts, so what evidence could be brought from the use of one or the other?!

Why did this practice spread to the US? It is implausible that there was newly heightened concern for the honor of Avraham Avinu. The universal practice in the United States is to write *ben/bat Avraham Avinu* for all converts in their *ketubah*s, and an Israeli Rabbinate official has confirmed to me that this is also the universal practice in Israel. With regard to Avraham Avinu's honor, what is the difference between a *get* and a *ketubah*?!

Rather, as the State of Israel became more central to world Judaism, American batei din realized that they needed their gittin to be accepted by the central Rabbanut bureaucracy. Somewhat ironically, they therefore became more likely to match the Rabbanut's officially prescribed procedures than the Rabbanut's own courts. This is true with regard to many issues.

Possibly some American dayyanim also meant to encode their qualms about specific conversions. But since they had other ways of conveying such concerns to fellow batei din, and because American batei din are generally horrified by attempts to invalidate conversions based on the converts' state of observance years later (at least since the Tropper/Eternal Jewish Family scandals became public), I assume that the majority simply wanted their gittin to "look normal" in Israel.

Converts are not told why the questions about observance are being asked. They are not told that honest answers may lead the Israeli Rabbinate to treat their divorce documents as evidence against the validity of their conversions. In many cases, the beit din itself may not realize this. But it is nonetheless true.

The Israeli nonprofit ITIM, headed by Rabbi Seth Farber, has repeatedly sued the Rabbinate to prevent them from using the divorce process as an occasion to reopen question of Jewish status. Doing so is now illegal, but it remains unclear whether the practice has ceased.

Regardless, there is no bar to the Rabbinate using the divorce documents of converts as evidence in an initial inquiry into Jewish status, such as when converts from abroad apply for Aliyah.

In other words, distinguishing between *"hager/hagiyoret"* and *"ben/bat Avraham Avinu"* in gittin puts converts in permanent danger of challenges to their own or their descendants' Jewishness.

American batei din have a moral obligation to return to the simple halakhah, which requires no such distinctions in the get, or at least to the narrow practice of the Toras Gittin.

We should regardless not be asking anyone about their religious practice when they come for divorce, all the more so converts, all the more so without being transparent about the stakes. Asking such questions raises anxieties in every convert about every imperfection in their halakhic practice and violates *ona'at hager*. We certainly must not continue a practice that raises unfounded doubts about many legitimate conversions, aids and abets those who seek to invalidate conversions we regard as perfectly legitimate, and makes many converts and their descendants permanently insecure.

When questions asked to rabbis read like movie scripts, should we suspect that they are?

Chapter 27

THE ART OF THE SHEILAH?

Law and limericks rarely mix. So I was astonished to run across the following introduction to a responsum from Rabbi Yitzchak Elchonon Spektor, perhaps the greatest Ashkenazi posek of the late 19th century:

A mostly frum lady named Etta
indulged in unhekhshered feta.
It was Ibsen's great play,
that led her astray,
so that day a rav called her Hedda.

The urgent question presented to R. Spektor was about the woman's divorce document. Obviously, it should have read עטא/Etta, but in fact read העדא/Hedda. A get must properly identify both parties to be valid. The husband had disappeared, so invalidating the get might make the woman an agunah for life. Yet could any reasonable person say that her name was "Hedda"?

R. Spektor was the international address for agunah questions, known for his broad shoulders, creativity, sensitivity, and diligence in resolving such issues. Rabbis referred their questions to him not as an abdication of responsibility but because they were confident that a permission from him would carry more weight than their own, and that there was no risk that he would forbid in any case where permission was possible. He did not disappoint in this case.

At first glance the gates of permission are locked with regard to this get, as this seems a case where the scribe "changed her name" from the one she is called by and uses as her autograph, and at first evaluation I see no clear permission because of the gravity of the issue. But with the help of G-d I now see that there is a way to permit her . .
.

R. Spektor points to a Beit Shmuel that validates a get that is written for someone who was given a nickname rather than an ordinary name at birth, say "Bill" instead of "William", even if one writes "William" in the get, so long as the vowels remain the same and everyone recognizes the relationship between the names. "Hedda" and "Etta" are close enough in the same way.

Here I need to confess: It was actually the other way around. The woman's name was "Hetta", and the get called her "Etta". I changed the facts to match the limerick, which of course is also my invention. Ibsen's Hedda Gabler opened in 1891, and R. Spektor's responsum is dated 5652=1892, but the get was written no later than 5650, and Etta presumably ate only *gevinat Yisroel* with a mehadrin hekhsher her entire life.

But here's the thing: the actual fact-pattern presented to Rav Elchonon contains many astonishing details that seem as halakhically irrelevant as Hetta's taste in cheese. So why include them?

Here is a (partial) plot outline, which will take up almost the rest of this essay:

Shabtai, a struggling alum of Slobodka Yeshiva, shows up at Chief Rabbi Mosheh Shimon Sivitz's door in Pittsburgh with a letter of introduction. Rabbi Sivitz offers Shabtai money. He refuses it, even though he isn't earning enough to support his wife and baby in Europe. What he wants instead is a daily chavrusa, because it's impossible to learn well by himself after a long day of hard and unremunerative work as a peddler. The chavrusa ends up involving much listening to moaning about economic failure and guilt.

A year later, Shabtai's wife and toddler arrive in America. They all come together to Rabbi Sivitz's house.

Rabbi Sivitz asks her: Why are you here?

She replies that her father sent her to America to ask for a divorce, because her husband simply can't support them, and she can't make enough on her own as a sheitelmacher to survive.

Rabbi Sivitz turns to Shabtai and asks: What do you want?

He replies, with his daughter clutching his hand, that he cannot bear the parting, but that his wife deserves the opportunity for a better life.

Rabbi Sivitz tells them to come back the next evening. If they still want the divorce, he will supervise it.

Meanwhile, he swings into action. An appeal to the local shochtim (kosher slaughterers) raises enough money to rent a nice apartment and stock it with food for a month, and more. The local day school needs a teacher. The local sheitelmacher has a job for someone with experience.

When the couple returns, he tells them that the get will be arranged in a different apartment. They look like prisoners being led off to jail as they follow him. There's a banquet in progress when they arrive, and he tells them to join in – we'll do the get afterward. The husband is honored with leading Grace after Meals, and only then does Rabbi Sivitz drop the news – This apartment is for you! You have jobs! Here's money you can invest! Ecstasy ensues. The couple lives happily ever after and becomes very wealthy.

Shabtai's sister works for a rich man in Boston. He pays her well enough that she has real savings, which she sends to Shabtai, who entrusts them to Rabbi Sivitz as capital for his free loan fund. One day, Shabtai shows up accompanied by an exceedingly handsome and broadly knowledgeable young man. The man introduces himself as a secretary working in the office of Andrew Carnegie, with a princely salary. Then Shabtai brings out his sister Hetta from Boston – Mazal tov! They're engaged!

But Hetta is as plain as her groom is handsome, and Rabbi Sivitz is suspicious. "Do you have any relatives here in Pittsburgh?" "No." "How long have you been here?" "One month". He calls over Shabtai and tells him: "Check this man out thoroughly, because I think he'll take Hetta's money and leave her an agunah!". Not a day passes before Shabtai appears and demands Hetta's money back then and there, because he's heard "rumors" that the rabbi has wasted it. The rabbi is forced to borrow from short-term lenders (read: usurers) to repay it. Shabtai then insists that the rabbi perform the wedding. Rabbi Sivitz tries to select invalid witnesses, telling Shabtai "It's for your sister's good, so I can *permit her when he leaves her an agunah!", but Shabtai thwarts his plans.*

Of course, the handsome groom is gone without a trace the next morning. Shabtai goes from rabbi to rabbi in town seeking sgulot (supernatural assistance), and follows all their esoteric instructions without fail – but to no avail. Finally, as a last desperate measure, he shows up at our author's door and insists: "You must give me a sgulah to bring her husband back for a get! If I sinned, why should my sister suffer?"

Rabbi Sivitz is fed up by now, and aside from that, does not believe in sgulot. But Shabtai won't leave! So he decides to have a little fun. He writes out a long prayer and hands it to Shabtai with the following instructions: "First, you must memorize this. Then, place it in your chumash facing the verses in Parashat Ki Teitzei setting out the get process. Then put your chumash in the Holy Ark. Every night between midnight and 2 am, go to the shul in the dark and put your head inside the Ark and recite this prayer. Tell no one what you are doing!" Shabtai finally leaves. Rabbi Sivitz assumes that he'll realize by the next day that this is ridiculous, and meanwhile at least he's out of the house.

Next week, Shabtai is arrested as a thief. People caught him breaking into shul after midnight! He tells Rabbi Sivitz that he's not bitter – it's just a little hard that people follow him wherever he goes, especially when he goes to shul at 1 every morning. But his sister matters above all, so he'll keep doing it. Rabbi Sivitz has nothing to say. He heads off to Cleveland for an extended business trip with a heavy heart.

On his return, his wife meets him at the door excitedly: "Did you hear? A rabbi in Baltimore sent a letter saying that a man showed up saying that he couldn't live with himself having left a woman an agunah in Pittsburgh, and he wanted a get right away, so please send the wife's names for the get immediately! You weren't here, so I asked R. Ploni to send the names, and he did, and here's Hetta's get!". Except of course that Hetta's get was written "Etta".

Reading this amazing story, I had to wonder. None of it matters halakhically other than the names and the reality that the woman would be an agunah if the get were invalidated. So why did Rabbi Sivitz write the whole story out?

Some of the Chavot Yair's fact-patterns seem similarly baroque (I am not the first to notice this), so perhaps there is an undiscovered genre of Rabbinic short stories. Maybe limericks will yet emerge.

Or maybe one really needs to write the full story, every time. Let me briefly explain why.

An Israeli rabbanut beit din some years ago heard the case of an American man who serially married Christian woman and absconded immediately with all the wedding gifts. He then discovered his Jewish heritage and moved to Israel, where he found a Jewish victim, and promptly vanished again overseas. She asked to have the marriage annulled as a *mekach taut*, a mistaken transaction. One *dayyan* argued that since Rav Yitzchok Elchonon (and Rabbi Sivitz, and Rabbi Yaakov Yosef of New York) all validated Hetta's questionable get rather than annulling her marriage, obviously they held that women would knowingly marry such scoundrels, and so annulment was impossible.

With Rabbi Sivitz's narrative in hand, we can easily reject the comparison. Rabbi Sivitz presumably warned Hetta via Shabtai, and she was persuaded to go ahead anyway. That case where a specific woman accepted a known risk cannot be generalized to one in which the marriage took place in perfect innocence, with no obvious way (I believe this was pre-Google) to investigate the groom's past career in a different country.

On the other hand, the rabbi citing the case had Rabbi Sivitz's narrative in hand; I followed his citation to L'veit Yaakov, Shu"t Uvirurei Halakhah #4. So I wonder in turn whether the summary in the rabbanut decision conveys the full facts of the case.

That Rabbanut decision also includes separate opinions from four rather than three *dayyanim*, and each opinion ends without an actual ruling. Some years later, one of the *dayyanim* went outside the rabbanut system and convened an ad hoc beit din for the purpose of issuing a leniency in a case with a similar but more detailed fact-pattern. Perhaps there is a plague of such wedding-jumpers, but I suspect that the story of that decision as well would make a fine film.

PART VI

BIBLICAL PORTRAITS

Did Hashem bless Yishmael only because Avraham insisted?

Chapter 28

PROPHECY AND MORAL DISCOMFORT

In Chapter 17 of Genesis, G-d speaks to Avram/Avraham five times. Four of those speeches are consecutive; the fifth follows Avraham's four-word plea "*Would that Yishmael live before You*". The speeches seem partially redundant. However, Rav Yosef Ibn Caspi explains that the entire chapter takes place in Avraham's mind. What are presented as G-d's words actually embody stages of Avraham's continually deepening intellectual engagement with an initial Revelation.

Ibn Caspi's reading of the chapter as a coherent internal dialogue is supported by two other literary points. First, the chapter has an envelope structure, with its beginning and end each reporting Avraham's age. Second, the first Revelation is preceded by Hashem appearing to Avraham, and the last is followed by "*G-d finished speaking with him, and G-d ascended from upon Avraham*"[17].

Let's assume with Ibn Caspi that prophets often need time and thought to fully understand their own prophetic experience. Every prophet is therefore to some extent נִיבָּא וְלֹא יָדַע מַה שֶׁנִּיבָּא, a conduit for the Divine who speaks more than they understand. On the other hand, most literary expressions of non-Mosaic prophecy are interpretations rather than reproductions. .

Ibn Caspi understands Avram's initial revelation as verbal = consisting of words. But certainly some prophetic experiences are pictorial, and some philosophers argue that only Mosheh was capable of experiencing revelation verbally. For example, the inaugural prophecies of Yeshayahu and Yirmiyahu appear to be descriptions rather than transcriptions. I think the best understanding of Sefer Yirmiyah is very

---

[17] Ibn Caspi's comments with my rough translation can be found at https://moderntoraleadership.wordpress.com/2021/10/13/draft-rav-yosef-ibn-caspi-on-prophetic-experience/

much akin to Ibn Caspi's understanding of Genesis 17; Yirmiyah spends his life trying to understand and convey one or maybe two fundamental revelations. He knows that G-d has appointed him a prophet of destruction, but also or regrowth. The tragedy of the book is that neither we nor he ever find out the underlying meaning of "*to build and to plant*".

There is at least one other model for explaining Genesis 17. Exodus 33:19 – 34:3 is similarly structured as four consecutive Divine responses to Mosheh's question הראני נא את כבודך = *Please show me your glory.* Professor Mosheh Bernstein taught me that these Divine responses (or at least the first three; I may have added the fourth) reflect increasing concessions as Mosheh stolidly refuses to react gratefully or joyously to G-d's responses.

"*I will cause all My goodness to pass before you etc.*"

(poker face).

"*You cannot see my Face, because no human can see Me and live!*"

(shrug).

"*Behold a place with Me etc.*"

(poker face).

"*Carve for yourself two tablets like the first ones.*"

(reaches for chisel).

In this model, consecutive reports of Divine communication reflect G-d *k'b'yakhol* changing His mind in response to human dissatisfaction.

Ibn Caspi might point to a key literary difference. In Exodus, we are given no description at all of how Mosheh reacts to G-d's initial communications. By contrast, Genesis 17 describes Avraham as falling on his face in response to the first Revelation, and as falling on his face and engaging in internal dialogue before responding verbally to the fourth Revelation. So perhaps the best approach is a hybrid. Avraham grows in understanding and also implicitly challenges G-d.

Let's begin to play out how such an approach might play out in our text. I look forward to your critiques of my attempt and especially your own interpretations of the text using this approach.

Here is the first Divine speech

אֲנִי־אֵ-ל שַׁ-דַּ֫י
הִתְהַלֵּ֣ךְ לְפָנַ֔י וֶהְיֵ֖ה תָמִֽים
וְאֶתְּנָ֥ה בְרִיתִ֖י בֵּינִ֣י וּבֵינֶ֑ךָ
וְאַרְבֶּ֥ה אוֹתְךָ֖ בִּמְאֹ֥ד מְאֹֽד:
I am E-l Shad-dai
Walk before Me and be tamim
and I will situate My covenant between Myself and you
and I will increase you very greatly.

This section has four key elements:
1. Identification of G-d
2. Avram's responsibilities
3. Covenant (possibly conditional on fulfillment of 2)
4. Growth.

Each of these elements is presented succinctly, but we don't yet know whether that brevity reflects clarity or confusion. For example, we don't know whether the term "Shad-dai" was previously familiar to Avram, or whether the idea of 'walking with G-d' had an experiential analog in either polytheistic religion or human relationships.

Let's examine if and how these same elements appear in the second, considerably longer, Divine speech.

אֲנִ֑י
הִנֵּ֥ה **בְרִיתִ֖י** אִתָּ֑ךְ
וְהָיִ֕יתָ לְאַ֖ב הֲמ֥וֹן גּוֹיִֽם׃
וְלֹא־יִקָּרֵ֥א ע֛וֹד אֶת־שִׁמְךָ֖ אַבְרָ֑ם וְהָיָ֤ה שִׁמְךָ֙ אַבְרָהָ֔ם
כִּ֛י אַב־הֲמ֥וֹן גּוֹיִ֖ם נְתַתִּֽיךָ׃
וְהִפְרֵתִ֤י אֹֽתְךָ֙ בִּמְאֹ֣ד מְאֹ֔ד וּנְתַתִּ֖יךָ לְגוֹיִ֑ם וּמְלָכִ֖ים מִמְּךָ֥ יֵצֵֽאוּ׃
וַהֲקִמֹתִ֨י אֶת־בְּרִיתִ֜י בֵּינִ֣י וּבֵינֶ֗ךָ וּבֵ֨ין זַרְעֲךָ֧ אַחֲרֶ֛יךָ לְדֹרֹתָ֖ם **לִבְרִ֥ית** עוֹלָ֑ם
לִהְי֤וֹת לְךָ֙ לֵֽא-לֹהִ֔ים וּֽלְזַרְעֲךָ֖ אַחֲרֶֽיךָ׃
וְנָתַתִּ֣י לְ֠ךָ֠ וּלְזַרְעֲךָ֨ אַחֲרֶ֜יךָ
אֵ֣ת ׀ אֶ֣רֶץ מְגֻרֶ֗יךָ אֵ֚ת כָּל־אֶ֣רֶץ כְּנַ֔עַן לַאֲחֻזַּ֖ת עוֹלָ֑ם
וְהָיִ֥יתִי לָהֶ֖ם לֵא-לֹהִֽים׃

I

behold My covenant with you
You will become father of a trove of nations.
Your name will no longer be called Avram; Your name will be Avraham
because I have situated you as father of a trove (av hamon) of
nations.
I will make you very greatly fruitful
I will situate you as nations
kings will emerge from you
I will establish My covenant between Myself and you
and between your descendants after you, for all their generations, as
an eternal covenant
to be for you an Elo-him, and for your descendants after you.
I will give to you and to your descendants after you
the land of your sojourning, the entire land of Canaan, as an eternal
homestead
and I will become for you an Elo-him.

1. Identification of G-d

Here G-d plainly eschews identification ("I am E-l Shad-dai" – "I")
in favor of description. The notion of being/becoming a relational Elo-
him may also be the key element of this. But it may be much of the
section expounds "Shad-dai".

2. Avram's responsibilities

This section contains no explicit mention of human responsibilities, although one might argue that becoming a relational E-lohim requires a partner. From a literary perspective, though, it seems more likely that the renaming of Avram to Avraham parallels the obligation to walk with G-d and be *tamim*. Perhaps being the "father of a trove of nations" implies responsibility for humanity.

3. Covenant (possibly conditional on fulfillment of 2)

G-d clarifies that the covenant is multigenerational and eternal (assuming that *berit olam* doesn't mean that it lasts only until the next Jubilee year). There is no mention of conditionality.

4. Growth.

Avraham will be very greatly fruitful, become many nations, and have royal descendants. It's not clear how the "nations" he will become relate to the "trove of nations" that he will be father to.

Overall, I think it would be reasonable in Ibn Caspi's framework to see this section as resulting primarily from intense meditation on the phrase "I will increase you very greatly", with the primary outcome being that "increase" refers to having many descendants. The promise of the Land responds to the pragmatic challenges of population growth.

The transformation of an individual into family into multiple nations inevitably carries with it profound moral challenges. These relate both to tensions among those descendants, as population growth may lead subgroup identities to become more powerful than the overall family, and between those descendants and others. There may be tension between the description of Avraham as a father of multiple nations, and the statement that his descendants will inherit only one land (remembering that the land was not large enough to hold Avraham and Lot together). It may be that Avraham needs to internalize the realities of his future before he can begin to deal with their moral implications.

The third Divine speech concretizes the covenant as circumcision. This is a human responsibility, and failure to circumcise is a nullification of the covenant. But I think the deeper significance of this section is that it makes clear that Avraham's descendants are intended and required to set themselves apart. He is not a universal father.

However, the obligation of circumcision also applies to males who are not biological or legal descendants = וּבֶן־שְׁמֹנַ֣ת יָמִ֗ים יִמּ֥וֹל לָכֶ֖ם כָּל־זָכָ֑ר לְדֹרֹתֵיכֶ֑ם יְלִ֣יד בָּ֔יִת וּמִקְנַת־כֶּ֙סֶף֙ מִכֹּ֣ל בֶּן־נֵכָ֔ר אֲשֶׁ֛ר לֹ֥א מִזַּרְעֲךָ֖ הֽוּא׃. So Avraham's descendants. This extension reminds me of Rav Yaakov Kaminetsky z"l's argument that Judaism would be racist if it did not allow for conversion.

The fourth Divine speech is entirely about Sarah. Why is she introduced at this point? Here Dr. Bernstein's approach in Exodus is especially valuable: the third speech must have left Avraham dissatisfied. The question is whether his dissatisfaction arose from a sense that Sarah had not been given a role as Foremother, or else because G-d's failure to mention Yishmael specifically left open the possibility that Yishmael was not a covenantal descendant. G-d's answer is oblique, so Avraham asks directly "If only Yishmael would live before You". G-d's response is a concession – "*Regarding Yishmael – I have heeded you*", and Yishmael is now promised a great but separate destiny. G-d leaves after speaking – it's not clear whether Avraham had more he wanted to say.

The overall thrust of this reading is that while Yishmael is circumcised, the dialogue surrounding the command of circumcision is the beginning of what Rav Amital z"l called *akeidat Yishmael*. Avraham does not immediately understand, and perhaps resists knowing, that his covenant with G-d will not extend to all his descendants. When G-d ended their conversation (or: when Avraham's understanding of his own prophetic experience plateaued), he still had questions about how his status as "father of a trove of nations" could be squared with Yishmael's non-covenantal destiny. Perhaps part of our human responsibility within the covenant is to keep asking those questions.

Chapter 29

THE AVRAHAM ACCORDS

Around the time of Yishmael's expulsion, the Philistine King Avimelekh came to Avraham, together which the head of his military, and proposed a treaty. *"G-d is with you in all that you do. Now swear to me etc.".* Avraham said: *"I will swear".* Then Avraham rebuked Avimelekh about the illegal and corrupt activities of his subordinates, and Avimelekh denied knowing anything about them. Then Avraham gave Avimelekh stuff for free, and they cut a deal/covenant. Sometime after that, G-d said to Avraham: *Take, please, your son, your unique one, who, you have loved, Yitzchak . . ."*

It's not clear why this story is in Torah. It seems to change nothing. Yitzchak copies his father's trick of passing his wife Rivkah off as his sister when he moves to Gerar, demonstrating his belief that there is still no fear of G-d in Philistia. The result is different only because Avimelekh is warier this time around. Also, Yitzchak finds his father's wells vandalized, and his own are vandalized as well, and eventually he is asked to leave.

We don't know for certain whether Avraham and Yitzchak's assessment of Philistia as a G-dfearless society is correct. Evidence for their view is that in Genesis 26:11, Avimelekh restrains his society by threatening the death penalty for maltreating *the man or his wife*, not simply by revealing that she is his wife. Also, his language *"hanogeia"* seems intended to recall the plague (*vayenaga)* that G-d sent in 12:17 for maltreating Sarah – perhaps one can have a society that fears G-d only in very narrow ways. Regardless, Avraham is willing to covenant with a society that he believes lacks all fear of G-d, in which visiting women can be confiscated by the monarch. Was that wrong of him?

Rashbam says that making the treaty was wrong. In a characteristically brute-force effort to explain why the Akeidah is introduced by "It happened after these things", Rashbam comments:

אף כאן,

180

"אחר הדברים" שכרת אברהם ברית לאבימלך,
לו ולנינו ולנכדו של אברהם,
ונתן לו שבע כבשות הצאן.
וחרה אפו של הק' על זאת,
שהרי ארץ פלשתים בכלל גבול ישראל,
והק' ציוה עליהם לא תחיה כל נשמה . . .
לכן והא-להים נסה את אברהם = קינתרו וציערו . .
בלומר:
נתגאיתה בבן שנתתיו
לכרות ברית ביניכם ובין בניהם,
ועתה לך והעלהו לעולה
ויראה מה הועילה כריתות ברית שלך.
So too here,
"after these things" means after Avraham cut a covenant with Avimelekh,
with him and running through his grandchildren and Avraham's,
and gave him the seven sheep.
The anger of the Holy Blessed One was kindled by this,
because the land of the Philistines was included within the boundary of Israel,
and G-d commanded regarding them "You must not leave any soul alive".
Therefore "and G-d tested Avraham", meaning that he harassed and afflicted him . . .
meaning:
You grew haughty regarding the son that I gave
to cut a covenant amongst you and their children
so now go bring him up as an *olah*
and we'll see what effect your covenant-cutting has

I experience Rashbam's reading as doing violence to the text. The Akeidah is not a punishment – that much at least is clear from G-d saying "please" at its outset. I like the argument that this episode is introduced with "*It happened at that same time*" specifically to exclude it from the general sequence of the narrative and to forestall Rashbam's argument (albeit it seems to have failed at that task). But discounting Rashbam's evidence, we are left with his opinion that making the treaty expressed a lack of faith.

This too fails to convince me. The Covenant Between the Pieces tells Avraham that his descendants will not inherit the Land until the fourth generation, and this covenant seems to run only for three generation rather than eternally (although *nin* and *nekhed* may not have their contemporary meaning here). Indeed, we can learn from the example of the Giv'onim that maintaining a sworn treaty commitment would have overridden the mitzvah of "*You must not leave any soul alive*", and yet no mention is made of any treaty with the Philistines when the Jews return to the Land after the interlude in Egypt.

In contrast to Rashbam, Rav Yaakov Kaminetsky (Emet l'Yaakov Genesis 21:2) expresses a positive view of both Avimelekh and the treaty, while retaining a deeply negative view of Philistine culture:

> What seems correct
> is that after the angel guaranteed that Yishmael would become a great nation,
> and it is mentioned in the name of the Zohar that it was in the merit of circumcision that Yishmael merited having the Land of Israel under his hand until the coming of the redeemer –
> therefore Scripture introduces Avraham's cutting the covenant with Avimelekh King of the Philistines, because no nation that is identified with lack of circumcision so much as the Philistines,
> as we find several times in Tanakh –
> see Judges 14:3 "to take a wife from among the daughters of the uncircumcised Philistines",
> and so also Judges 15:18, 1 Samuel 14:6 and 31:4, 2 Samuel 1:20, 2 Chronicles 10:4 –
> so we see that the Philistines symbolize the uncircumcisedness in the world,
> but nonetheless Avraham did not refrain from cutting a covenant with their king,
> because he was an *ish yashar* = "man of integrity",
> which shows that circumcision is not the main thing . . .

Note however that the covenant mentions nothing whatsoever about Avraham's relationship with the Philistine people. It seems to be a personal alliance with the rulers of an immoral society. The truth is that even Rashbam criticizes the treaty only because it reflects a lack of faith, not because it reflects an accommodation with evil.

How can we square all this with Avraham's inspiring refusal in 14:23 to accept anything from the King of Sodom "*so that you will not (be able to) say: I made Avraham wealthy*"? I see at least three fundamental approaches:

1) Sodom was much worse than Gerar, and its king was no different than any of his subjects. In this regard, it is worth reflecting on the king's non-appearance in the subsequent story of Lot and the angels. It is also worth reflecting on the reality that much of Avraham's wealth came from the King of Mitzrayim's gifts after his own mistreatment of Sarah.

2) Unlike Avimelekh, the King of Sodom did not ask for a covenant of mutual interest, but rather sought to bribe Avraham.

3) Avraham regretted his decision about Sodom, and deliberately acted differently with regard to Avimelekh and Gerar.

The third approach seems most attractive to me, as follows: After the destruction of Sodom, Avraham realized that non-engagement had been a disaster. Perhaps he should have taken both the people and the money, and tried to build a better society! Not having that option in Gerar, he decided that maintaining some form of *realpolitik* influence was worth the cost of being tarnished by association.

But the Torah never tells us how this calculation worked out. Maybe Avraham's influence kept Gerar from becoming Sodom. Or maybe engagement is worthwhile, and nation-building possible, only when you have the capacity to completely redo an evil but defeated society, and here Avraham became an unintentional accessory to evil.

In both foreign policy and individual relationships, there is no sure way to maximize the good when dealing with evil, and the Torah does not pretend otherwise. Effective policy may depend on many characteristics of those involved other than their goodness or evil, and on overall context.

Recognizing this complexity does not mean that there is no space for impassioned advocacy, as for example Rabbi Avidan Freedman's campaign against Israeli arms sales to human rights abusers. I don't know which/whether today's covenantal partners are parallel to Sodom,

Gerar, or Avraham's genuine friends Aner, Eshkol, and Mamrei, or something else entirely. But I'm grateful to be challenged to think about it.

Is it moral to "win" a negotiation?

Chapter 30

WHY AVRAHAM OVERPAID, AND IN CASH

Avraham paid for the field and cave in Chevron with "*400 shekels of silver* **oveir lasocheir**" = "negotiable currency". Why does the Torah bother to convey the mode of payment? Lest you suggest that there were tax implications - the transaction took place literally in full view of the local authorities. Avraham was not trying any fancy accounting.

Bereshit Rabbah (Lekh Lekha) asserts that four men – Avraham, Yehoshua, King David, and Mordekhai, each "yatza lahem monitin baolam", meaning that they minted distinctive coins that were widely accepted as negotiable currency. So perhaps the Torah means that Avraham used his own coins.

Why would that matter? Having one's coinage accepted is a common halakhic definition of sovereignty, for example with regard to the rule *dina demalkhuta dina*. The common denominator among the three aside from David seems to be that each was halakhically considered a sovereign despite not being a crowned king. Mentioning Avraham's currency thus validates the claim of Avraham's Hittite interlocutors that he is treated as a *nasi* in their midst (unless *nasi elo?im* has a purely religious meaning).

The midrash, and a beraita on Bava Kamma 67b, go so far as to report the design of Avraham's coins.

> There were four who had their coinage go out in the world:
> Avraham –
> *"... I will enlarge your reputation/שמך"*
> = his *monitin* went out. What was it?
> An elderly man and an elderly woman on one side, and a lad and a lass on the other side.

Rishonim discuss whether/why such images are forbidden, or scandalous even if permitted; perhaps they were busts rather than full-body portraits, or concave rather than raised, or perhaps the beraita meant only that these coins had the words *zaken/zkeinah/bachur/betulah* on them. They also debate whether the lad and lass represent Yitzchak and Rivkah, or rather Avraham and Sarah after their miraculous rejuvenation (which assumes that Avraham was also rejuvenated). But there is consensus that the elderly couple represents Avraham and Sarah. If we take this as fact, Avraham's use of these coins to purchase Sarah's grave seems especially meaningful.

But it is not generally a good idea to take this sort of midrash as fact. Moreover, archaeology poses a challenge to this interpretation. The oldest formal "coin" so far found is from more than a millennium after Avraham.

Aware of this issue, Rav Dovid Tzvi Hoffman (1843-1921) writes in his Commentary that "it appears that there were not minted coins then, but there were silver ingots, which perhaps had their weight engraved on them". Rabbi Hoffman's explanation anticipates by at least a century an article from the May 2021 issue of the Journal of Archaeological Science, which reports that "hoards" of Bronze Age metal all across Europe were often broken into units or multiples of standard weights, suggesting that they were used as a medium of exchange.

There is still no record of minted coins. But aside from the general weakness of archaeological arguments from absence, the underlying interpretation we've offered requires only that Avraham's endorsement of a currency was accepted without cavil – the midrashic add-on that his coins were minted, with an elaborate and distinctive decoration, is unnecessary.

On this reading, the Torah includes the detail of *oveir lasocher* in order to show that G-d had at least partially fulfilled His initial promise to Avraham at the outset of Lekh Lekha.

Malbim offers a radically different explanation:

So that he would not be able to make any claim of *ona'ah*

Cash makes the transaction final and irreversible and impervious to subsequent claims of unfairness. But who insisted on cash? The Torah does not tell us that Efron made any such demand. It seems that Avraham was afraid that Efron would renege. Why?

Malbim provides a wonderfully baroque reading of the story, in which Avraham must negotiate with different constituencies within the Hittites, and ensure that each understands his words differently. I suggest a simpler version.

The Hittites never had any intention of selling Avraham an *achuzat kever* = hereditary crypt, at any price. They were happy to give him any non-hereditary spot, and they genuinely respected him as an individual, so long as he was a wandering or visiting Jew. But they also knew – perhaps word of the 'Covenant Between the Pieces' had gotten around – that Avraham saw his descendants as the heirs to currently Hittite lands. They had no interest in legitimizing this perspective.

Chazal note that Hittites are not Semites, and that the various Canaanite groups in Bereishis all arrived recently as conquerors. But they saw themselves as justified in resisting Avraham.

Still, the diplomatic niceties had to be observed. Avraham personally was admired and perhaps also feared. So their first strategies were

1. Offer him everything he wants, just make sure there are no long-term implications.

2. Negotiate with him collectively, not individually, to avoid 'Prisoner's Dilemma' situations.

Avraham moves to negotiate with Efron individually, albeit still in public. The Hittites have no good reason to deny him this, but while ordinary Hittites know the overall strategy, they probably haven't been given specific coaching. Efron therefore makes an excusable but fatal error in the subsequent negotiations. He names a price that everyone present knows is absolutely, totally, incredibly ridiculous – but still, it is a price, and for Avraham, the land is literally priceless. So Avraham, without a word, takes out cash and pays asking price. What could Efron say? What could anyone say?

You've probably noticed that this narrative bears a family resemblance to pre-1948 and ongoing narratives about Jewish land purchases in Israel. So we need to discuss that before going on with our regularly scheduled Torah programming.

I'm open to at least five sorts of responses.

1. This isn't a compelling or even plausible reading of the text, and/or I prefer one of the other readings.

2. This is a plausible reading of the text, but the analogy to modern events is weak

3. This is a plausible reading of the text, but I don't see why the analogy to modern events should bother me, as I find Avraham's behavior throughout impeccable.

4. This would be a plausible reading of the text if it didn't cast troubling implications for modern events. But since it does, and since it is certainly not the only or even the most plausible reading, I don't think it should be treated as more than a clever *hava amina*.

5. This is a plausible reading of the text, but the analogy to modern events works both ways, and should give us a broader perspective on the episode. For example: what happens to Efron and his family the day after, and what does that tell us about Hittite culture? Why is G-d so sure that their "sin will be complete" within four generations?

Commentators over the centuries have disputed whether or not Efron's price reflects the real estate market at the time. My reading posits that the price was above-market. If it was worth more to Avraham than to anyone else, was it immoral of Efron to demand more from him?

I focused on the negotiation-narrative this week not because I was looking for narrow contemporary relevance, but rather because I'm learning the sixth chapter of Bava Metzia with a wonderful chaburah at YI Sharon. (You can find recordings of the weekly shiur at https://www.podpage.com/taking-responsibility-for-torah/category/employeremployee-law/.)

The position initially presented in the opening sugya of that chapter assumes that any labor contract freely agreed to is both halakhically binding and hashkafically just; a position presented afterward contends that such a contract may be halakhically binding and yet leave grounds for moral complaint, perhaps specifically if the economically weaker party ends up with less than the stronger party would have been willing to pay. That made me wonder whether my general discomfort with bargaining (in person, but not so much online) had a moral dimension; and that in turn made me wonder whether we should be rooting for Avraham to win the negotiations with the Hittites, or rather for the two sides to find an equilibrium position that reflects a "just" outcome.

More generally, does/should halakhah favor fixed, transparent pricing over the *shuk*? For example, some of my friends argue that unless job advertisements include a fixed salary, women will be offered and accept less than men for the same work. (Libertarian economists presumably counter that if true, this would lead to only women being hired; this is not the right context for that conversation.) If we favor the *shuk*, is that because fixed prices are too likely to create market distortions, or because we think that many people find bargaining a pleasurable experience?

My hope is that this essay succeeds in modeling a process of thinking about life through Torah rather than imposing our thoughts about life on Torah.

The difference between laughing at, laughing with, and making laugh

Chapter 31

YITZCHAKNESS

וישב יצחק בגרר.
וישאלו אנשי המקום לאשתו. ויאמר: "אחותי היא",
כי ירא לאמר "אשתי", 'פן יהרגני אנשי המקום על רבקה, כי טובת מראה
היא'.
ויהי כי ארכו לו שם הימים,
וישקף אבימלך מלך פלשתים בעד החלון וירא,
והנה – יצחק מצחק את רבקה אשתו!
Yitzchak settled in Gerar.
The people of the place asked I'his wife, and he said: "She is
my sister",
because he was afraid to say "my wife",
'lest the people of the place will kill me over Rivkah, because she is
good-looking'.
It happened when his days there were extended,
that Avimelekh King of the Pelishtim overlooked at the window and
saw,
behold – Yitzchak *metzachek et* Rivkah his wife!

"Yitzchak *metzachek*". Puns are notoriously untranslatable. But are
there ideas that can only be expressed via wordplay, so that one loses not
only art but essence in translation? On the other hand, are we be
comfortable saying that some literary devices in Chumash serve purely
artistic purposes?

Wordplays on *tz'ch'k* have already been prominent in Yitzchak's
story. Avraham (17:17) and Sarah (18:12) each *tz'ch'k* when told of his
impending birth; G-d responds to Avraham by revealing Yitzchak's
name, and to Sarah by asking Avraham why she had *tz'ch'ked*. Sarah
demands Yishmael's expulsion after seeing him *metzachek* (21:9). But
it's never clear why *tz'ch'k* is so important.

I don't have a satisfying explanation for why G-d reacts so
differently to Avraham than to Sarah. But it seems likely to me that
Yishmael is expelled for challenging the place of Yitzchak: *metzachek* =

making himself like Yitzchak. (That leads us to consider whether Lot seeming like a *metzachek* in the eyes of his sons in-law (19:14) explains why he failed to become Avraham's heir.) It follows plausibly that Yitzchak in our episode is revealing his essence = his Yitzchakness = the reason that he rather than Yishmael is Avraham's true heir.

But what is that essence? Answering this question requires a narrative and lexicographic excursus.

Narratively, the most pressing questions in our episode may be why Avimelekh was at the window, and why Yitzchak was so careless as to be caught. My suggested answer to the first is that Avimelekh never believed Yitzchak – many years ago, I framed this in class at Maimonides as

Eyes were rolling all over Philistia – "It's another of those Hebrews with their 'sisters'.

Note also that Yitzchak is not besieged by suitors for Rivkah. Perhaps Rivkah was in fact not unusually attractive to anyone but Yitzchak, and Yitzchak realized over time that no one cared whether she was his wife rather than his sister. However, it seems to me more likely that Avimelekh never believed the "sister" story. Why, then, was Yitzchak careless? Well, it had been a long time, and people usually relax their vigilance over time.

Here the lexicographic excursus may be helpful. What does "*metzachek*" mean? As with many words, it can but does not necessarily have a sexual connotation. Thus Potiphar's wife complains that her husband has brought a Hebrew slave "*letzachek banu*", which likely means "to make us the object of his sexual play". It is plausible that the Jews who "arose *letzachek*" during the Golden Calf_episode were erotically engaged. _

Yitzchak is *metzachek et*, and Yishmael is *metzachek*. Let's assume that these uses are at least erotically tinged. I suggest that *metzachek et* nonetheless does not mean, as most translations have it, "*sporting with*", or even as Everett Fox's more comprehensive "*laughing-and-loving with*". Both these assume that "*et*" here means "with", rather than serving as a direct object marker. I would instead have "was causing Rivkah his wife flirtatious laughter", or as Deborah Klapper suggested, "was making Rivkah giggle". In other words: What made Yitzchak who he was – in contrast to Yishmael and the Calf-worshipers, who were tz'ch'k for themselves, and in even starker contrast to the stereotype drawn by Mrs. Potiphar of one who is tz'ch'k others-as-objects – was that his tzchk was for the sake of another. Yitzchak did not grow careless – rather, he responded to Rivkah's need for affection.

Alternatively, Deborah suggests that Yitzchak was not being consciously erotic. Rather, just as his birth caused tz'ch'k for everyone who heard of it, being around him caused tzchk for Rivkah in a way which made it evident that he was her husband.

This reading of Yitzchak's character fits well with interpretations of Yitzchak praying lenokhakh ishto as "for the sake of his wife", and not so well with those that translate "lenokhach" as "opposite".

However, Yitzchak and Rivkah seem to develop serious communication issues as the years pass. Rivkah never discusses the behavior of her unborn children with Yitzchak, before or after she goes to inquire of Hashem. Yitzchak does not discuss his plans for blessing their sons with Rivkah. Rivkah obviously does not discuss her substitution of Yaakov for Esav with her husband.

It is tempting to connect veRivkah shoma'at (27:5) = Rivkah hearing Yitzchak instruct Esav, with vcSarah shoma'at (18:10) = Sarah hearing the angel tell Avraham that she will become pregnant and give birth. I assume that the angel **intended** Sarah to hear, knowing perfectly well that she was on the other side of the entrance. Perhaps Yitzchak intended Rivkah to overhear his initial conversation with Esav about the blessing, and to overwrite him if she thought it necessary, and their communication was complex but clear.

Targum 'Yonatan' accepts the connection to Sarah but draws an opposite conclusion: Rivkah overheard Yitzchak via ruach hakodesh, presumably even though Yitzchak tried to keep her from knowing. However, Or HaChayyim argues that shoma'at describes a continual state rather than a specific act:

מודיע הכתוב כי רבקה נביאה היתה
ושומעת תמיד בדברי יצחק וגו',

הגם שלא ידבר בפניה.
והבן.
*Scripture conveys that Rivkah was a prophetess
and continually heard Yitzchak's words etc.,
even those he did not speak in her presence.
Understand this.*

Or HaChayyim does not clarify whether Yitzchak was aware that he had no secrets from Rivkah, or whether he could equally hear her words. If the transparency was mutual, then of course he heard Rivkah's instructions to Yaakov as well.

The theoretical and practical challenges of telepathic relationships have to my knowledge been treated more extensively in secular than in Jewish literature, although there are interesting discussions around Amos 3:7: *"For Hashem Elokim will not do anything without revealing His secret to His servants the prophets",* sometimes in conjunction with or contradistinction from 18:17: *"Hashem said: Am I concealing from Avraham that which I am doing?"* And maybe neither Rivkah nor Yitzchak had yet developed this ability as of their sojourn in Gerar. So we can wonder if their relationship remained one which brought *tz'ch'k* to Rivkah simply from Yitzchak's presence, and which brought out Yitzchak's essence. It's also fair to note that the Torah never tells us anything regarding the meaning or significance of Rivkah's name. This makes it hard for us to get a full picture of her contribution.

My preference is for readings that present Yitzchak and Rivkah as true minds, and admit no impediments to the constancy of their love. To be taken seriously, any such reading requires accepting the equality of husband and wife, and recognizing that love does not require full agreement.

A Nonmusical Tale of Two Brides for Two Brothers

Chapter 32

LAVAN AND YAAKOV IN THEIR OWN WORDS

Lavan:

It's been a month. I can't deny my obligation to feed my sister's son, but it doesn't seem fair that he spends all his time learning Torah (if that's really what he's doing; it's not clear to me why he left yeshiva[1] if that's all he wants out of life) while everyone else is working. My own sons are grumbling. Maybe a subtle hint would do it? I could pretend that he was already doing work I should pay him for, and ask him to name his own salary. Then once he's named it – I think he's unlikely to cheat by setting it at an unreasonable level - I'll have a basis for demanding accountability.

Lavan said to Yaakov: Can you be my brother, and yet serve me for free?! Tell me your usual salary!

Yaakov:

It's been a month. My mother sent me here to be safe. She was sure Uncle Lavan would protect me from my brother. But she also warned me to thoroughly examine the teeth of any horse he tries to gift me.

So here's what I think he's up to.

His workers don't live anywhere near as well as I do right now. Agreeing to a salary as an employee would be setting a firm and much lower cap on his obligations, probably without any corresponding limit on mine. Even admitting that I have a standard salary would dramatically lower my social position. This could even be a test to see whether I deserve his respect.

At the same time, I feel guilty not working. This is not one of those Zevulun-Yisso(s)cher relationships; it's more as if an alcoholic religious minority held the swing vote in a democracy and forced the majority to buy them lots of single-malt scotch.

I have an idea! My cousin Rachel is beautiful, and I really wouldn't mind marrying her when I'm properly settled. She's also younger (did I mention prettier? And **much** more cheerful?) than Leah. What if I told

Uncle Lavan that I'd work for him for, say, seven years, in exchange for marrying Rachel?

Let's think this through carefully. There's a chance he'll say yes. If so, then I won't be an employee, but rather still family – even closer family! and he'll have to support me for seven years in the manner to which I've become accustomed. And at the end of that, he'll have to give me her dowry, and she really is beautiful, so all that would be great.

Now he might say no because Leah isn't married yet, and it would be cruel to have her be the bridesmaid at a younger sister's wedding. But that's not a big deal - in seven years I'm sure that she will be married (although despite the old family joke about two brides for two brothers, I don't think that Esav is the man for her, and anyways I don't think he'll be talking to Lavan as long as I'm here).

Worst comes to worst, he says no, and then I've offered, and he still has to support me and treat me as family. Well, real worst-case scenario he somehow finds a way to have me marry Leah instead. So I'll try and specify Rachel as carefully and redundantly as I can[2].

Yaakov loved Rachel; He said: I will serve you for seven years in exchange for Rachel, your daughter, the younger one.

Lavan:

That was really clever! I underestimated him. I wonder if my sister warned him about me?

Meanwhile, a lot can happen in seven years, and perhaps I see a way to save Leah from that brute Esav. I really don't want her crying like this for the rest of her life[3].

Lavan said: It is better, my giving her to you, than my giving her to another man: stay put with me.

Yaakov:

That went by faster than I had thought possible. I really appreciate Uncle Lavan taking care of all the arrangements, and paying for both the florist and the band, and the people here really seem to love the open bar! But this local custom of the groom drinking a l'chaim with every guest seems a little excessive, especially for someone who doesn't usually drink except for kiddush.

Yaakov said to Lavan: Produce my wife, because my time is completed; and I will go in to her . . .
What have you done to me! It was for Rachel that I served you; why did you deceive me?

Lavan:
It cannot be done that way in our place, to give the younger before the elder.
Also, you forgot to specify the woman this time.
Complete this week - that one as well is given you for the service you will serve with me, seven other years.
Leah is your wife now, and you are responsible to maintain her social status.

Yaakov:
Thoughts the night before a wedding
Eisav's shadow lingers in her eyes;
every time we mate
I become the brother I despise[4].
My birthright, my blessing, and my wife
belong to him, so I hate
everything of value in my life
except Rachel, who loved me at first sight.
The wild dreams of love-crazed youth
are mine again tonight
transforming beauty into truth
desire into right.
Leah deserves more,
but this week's wait
seemed longer than the seven years before.
And the past seven years felt even longer, because I had nothing to look forward to except leaving. I don't believe that Lavan will ever give me anything but promises and daughters.
I must remember not to agree to anything. But it burns me up to let him get away with this.
I don't think he has any excuse to keep me here now that Rachel has given birth. But I must remember not to agree to anything.
It happened that after Rachel gave birth to Yosef, that Yaakov said to Lavan: Send me away, and I will go, to my place and to my land. Give

my wife and my children, whom I have served you in exchange for them, and I will go, because you know the service that I have served you, and Hashem blessed you in my footsteps. But now, when do I get to prosper my own home?

Lavan:
The truth is that he's been a good husband to Rachel, and in some ways a better husband to Leah, and we've all prospered. Bilhah and Zilpah seem okay as well. On the other hand, maybe he didn't really want Rachel to get pregnant – the only time I've ever heard him raise his voice was when she demanded children. Do you suppose I could get him to agree to another multiyear contract in exchange for another woman?
Lavan said to him: Please, if I have found favor in your eyes; I have divined that Hashem has blessed me for your sake.
(Yaakov does not respond.)
He said: Nakvah[5] your price upon me, and I will give it.

Yaakov:
That was quite a dig: I have more than enough women, thanks to him. Regardless, he makes it very clear that I take nothing with me if I leave. Even if he changes his mind and decides to be generous, he'll hold it over me forever that I owe him, and I'm obviously not good at resisting. I really wish I could prevent him from saying "I made Yaakov rich"[6], when really it's the other way around. Maybe he doesn't know about recessive genes?
He said: You know the service I have done for you, and how your flocks were with me. The little that was before me waxed and became a multitude, and Hashem blessed you as my associate; but now, when will I also do for my house?
He said: What can I give you?
He said: You will give me nothing! If you do this thing for me, I will return, shepherd your flocks, guard ...

Two Jewish encounters with Esav

Chapter 33

Confidence-Building Measures in Biblical Foreign Policy

On his way back to Canaan from Aram,

"Yaakov sent mal'akhim (messengers or angels)
before him to Esav his brother, toward Seir, the fields of Edom,
as follows:
"So you must say to my master, to Esav:
'So says your servant Yaakov . . .'"
(Bereishis 33:4-5).

On Yaakov's descendants' way back to Canaan from Mitzrayim,

"Mosheh sent mal'akhim
from Kadesh to the King of Edom:
'So says your brother Israel . . .'".
(Bamidbar 20:14)

The parallel is striking. But in Bereishis it is the narrator who describes Esav as Yaakov's brother, while Yaakov refers to Esav as his master. By contrast, Mosheh himself presents Israel and Edom as brothers and as equals.

The outcomes are also different.

While Yaakov's *mal'akhim* initially report that Esav is on his way with 400 (presumably armed and bellicose) men, the brothers' physical encounter ends in a rapprochement. Esav then departs Canaan in favor of Yaakov.[18]

---

[18] Esav suggests that he and Yaakov travel together, but Yaakov replies that he would come to Seir eventually. The valence of Yaakov's reply and its connection to the episode in Bamidbar are beyond the scope of this essay.

By contrast, when Edom responds to Bnei Yisroel's second message with a curt "No" and a visible display of force, Bnei Yisroel change their plans and take a circuitous route to Canaan that avoids Edom.

The simplest way of accounting for these differences is to say that Edom/Esav acknowledged Yaakov/Bnei Yisroel's absolute right to Canaan, but in turn demanded recognition of their own equal authority over Seir. This can plausibly be called "The Two State Solution", with Esav firmly believing that good fences make good neighbors.

This approach deliberately avoids asking the kind of questions that would necessitate more nuance. For example, it assumes that Mosheh and Bnei Yisroel's words and actions were irrelevant to Edom's response.

We can be more imaginative. Mosheh could have copied Yaakov's policy by sending a massive caravan of gifts along with his messengers. Bnei Yisroel might have divided their camp in half, and sent one half forward (including women and children) to kneel before the King of Edom. Would Edom have responded graciously?

Maybe Mosheh and Bnei Yisroel had real agency here.

Or maybe Edom would have seized the opportunity for demigenocide.

Yaakov had no way around Esav. His only alternative was permanent landlessness and never reaching his father's house. Risking heavy casualties was a reasonable choice for him. By contrast, Mosheh and Bnei Yisroel had the option of avoiding confrontation by taking a much less convenient route. They had no need to take large risks for the mere possibility of peace.

Netziv finds a third way. Mosheh had agency here, but he had no genuine interest in traversing Edom. Rather, his goal was to empower Edom. His message was literally a confidence-building measure. Moreover, Mosheh had to accomplish this without letting Bnei Yisroel understand his purpose. Here is Netziv, followed by my translation:

אמנם עוד יש בזה דבר עמוק,
שהרי אנו רואים דשליחות הראשון כתיב וישלח משה,
ושליחות שניה כתיב ויאמרו אליו בני ישראל,

אלא באמת ידע משה היטב כי לא יאבה מלך אדום, כמו שאמר לו ה *'כי לא אתן*

לכם מארצו עד מדרך כף רגל,

אבל משום שאמר ה' למשה

ויראו מכם ונשמרתם מאד ,

והיה בזה המצוה להשמר שלא ייראו

והיו בטוחים שלא בבח ישראל לעבור עליהם בעל כרחם,

על כן עשה משה זה השליחות

כדי שיבין מלך אדום שתלוי ברצונו,

וכיון שענה מלך אדום *פן בחרב אצא לקראתך* -

ידע משה שסר פחד ישראל ממנו, ושוב לא שלח אליו,

אבל בני ישראל – הוסיפו לנסות,

ומשום הבי לא רצה משה לשלח אנשי ישראל,

שמא יראו השלוחים כמה המה נפחדים ונמוגים,

כאשר כן היה באמת,

והיו ישראל מתאמצים ללכת בלי פחד מחרב אדום,

והיה צריך למשה להלוך נגד רוחם,

על כן ראה לשלוח מאומות העולם

שלא שמו לב כי אם לדעת תשובת המלך,

והיו סבורים ישראל שבאמת לבם ברי עליהם,

ושוב לא עלה על לב להלוך בעל כרחם

. . .

עבור בגבולו -

העיד הכתוב שלא בשביל איזה טעם מיאן,

אלא לא רצה שיעברו בגבולו,

והיינו משנאה כבושה לא עשה להם טובת הנאה

There is something else deep here,

because regarding the first agency it writes *And Mosheh sent*,

but regarding the second *Bnei Yisroel said to him.*

The truth is that Mosheh knew well that the King of Edom would not agree,

as Hashem had said to him (Devarim 2:5) *I will not give you from his land even a footfall.*

However, because Hashem said to Mosheh (D'varim 2:4):

They will be in terror of you, be very careful,

meaning a commandment to be careful (to ensure) that Edom not be in terror,

and that they be secure that Israel would not use force to traverse their territory against their will,

therefore Mosheh did this sending

> **so that the King of Edom would understand that all depended on his will.**
> Once the king of Edom replied *lest I go out to greet you with the sword,*
> Mosheh knew that fear of Israel had departed from him, and he no longer sent (messages) to him.
> But Bnei Yisroel made a further try.
> Mosheh therefore did not want to send Jews,
> lest the agents see that the Edomites were in fact afraid and trembling,
> as was in fact the case,
> and the Jew were stubbornly insisting on going through without fear of Edom's sword,
> and Mosheh had to oppose the spirit of the people.
> Therefore he sent non-Jewish agents, who cared only to hear the words of the king's response,
> so the Jews would think that the Edomites were actually stouthearted,
> and thus they no longer thought of traversing against their will.
>
> . . .
>
> "Pass within his boundaries" –
> Scripture testifies that Edom refuses not because of a genuine rationale,
> but rather he simply did not wish them to traverse within his boundaries,
> meaning that because of a deep-seated hatred he would not give them even a costless benefit.

Netziv argues that the *mal'akhim* that Mosheh sends to Edom are neither angels nor Jewish – rather, Mosheh sends residents of the place where Bnei Yisroel are staying: "*Mosheh sent mal'akhim **who were** from Kadesh to the King of Edom.*" Mosheh fully expects the Edomites to respond angrily.[19]

---

[19] Talmud Pesachim 113b tells the story of a single witness who testifies in court about someone else's sin, and is whipped for defamation, since a single witness can have no legal effect. He protests: "Tovah sinned, and Zygud is whipped?" Talmud Makkot 11a suggests

More convincingly, Netziv notes that while Mosheh sends the initial agents, it is Bnei Yisroel as a whole who respond to Edom's refusal. His explanation is that Bnei Yisroel were unaware that Mosheh wanted and expected the negotiations to fail.

I have a suggestion that builds on Netziv.

The Torah places the dialogue with Edom immediately after the episode of the Waters of Controversy, which ends with Mosheh and Aharon being denied entry to Canaan. Chazal interpret this juxtaposition as emphasizing Mosheh's egoless leadership:

> In the ordinary way of the world,
> if a person engages in business with a fellow and loses thereby,
> he separates from him and wishes not to see him;
> but Mosheh,
> even though he was punished because of Benei Yisroel,
> he did not unload their burden from his shoulders".

This explanation pays no heed to an apparent thematic connection. Mosheh's punishment was the result of Bnei Yisroel's excessive worry about water, and the negotiations with Edom center around water. *"We will not drink well-water"*. *"If we drink your water, I and my cattle, I will pay their sale price"*. The goal seems to be to ensure that Bnei Yisroel will not ever again be dependent on miracles for water.

Perhaps the second message is from Bnei Yisroel rather than from Mosheh because his political power waned once everyone knew that a leadership transition would soon be necessary, especially regarding water. I wonder whether Netziv's portrait of Mosheh as leader casting a veil over his own actions and keeping his constituents in the dark about his goal seems proper and ethical to us.

But I'm also reflecting on Netziv's understanding that G-d commanded us not only to leave Edom's sovereignty over its land intact,

---

that this is a folk proverb rather than a historical report. Onkelos translates *mal'akhim* here as "izgadin", because the Aramaic root z g d means "messenger". So the Talmudic proverb may actually be an early version of "Don't shoot the messenger!"

but also to ensure that Edom felt secure about our intentions. I'm fascinated that Mosheh Rabbeinu interpreted this as requiring proactive measures to build Edom's self-confidence. That self-confidence could be based only on feeling secure about our intentions and not on actual military parity. The key threat to G-d's policy came from Jews who could not understand why might did not make right so long as we were not seizing land permanently.

All this because Edom is our brother, whom we must not abominate, even though he continues to cultivate his hatred for us and expresses this hatred by choosing lose-lose over win-win propositions. Was the hatred grounded in a contention that Esav's departure from Canaan was involuntary, or at the least insufficiently considered? Do Mosheh and G-d think that their policy will eventually diminish Edom's hatred?

Not so long ago, in our very own galaxy, even raising the last possibility might have seemed silly blue-skying. And yet the Roman Catholic Church, which our tradition often identifies with Edom, has changed dramatically, almost unimaginably, on anti-Semitism in the past 60 years. So perhaps there are lessons to learn here, and to consider applying, with enormous caution, to relationships with other relatives.

Strange as it seems, there's been a run of crazy dreams,
and a man who can interpret could go far, could become a star.

Chapter 34

ON THE INTERPRETATION OF DREAMS

On his way to Lavan's house, Yaakov dreams of angels ascending and descending (28:11-15). But after fourteen-plus years in Lavan's house, he dreams of sheep ascending each other (31:10-13). His last dream ends with G-d commanding him "*Get up and leave this land, and return to your birthland (מולדתך)*".

The last sentence ironically reverses G-d's initial command to Avram (לך לך מארצך וממולדתך). This shows that the family has progressed. Unlike Avram, Yaakov has a cultural backstop, a morally usable past. On the other hand, it appears to track Yaakov's personal decline. Deborah often quotes Rabbi David Silber as saying that when your dream-subjects shift from angels to copulating sheep, it's time to "*Get up and leave this land*".

But Rabbi Silber may have overstated Yaakov's decline. Dreams may reflect Divine interventions from without, or may result of internal promptings. Yaakov's dream-perspective pulls back from the sheep until he can see the projector and notice the angelic operator, who in turn identifies as the G-d of his previous dream ("*I am the E-l of Beit E-l*")[20], and holds him to his prior commitments ("*where you made an oath to Me*"). Maybe all that matters is that Yaakov retains the spiritual capacity to let G-d in.

In fact, Yaakov's dream-visions always include the director's commentary. By contrast, his son Yosef dreams in full naivete. Interpretation happens only after Yosef wakes up. Even though he declares piously that "*after all, interpretations are G-d's*" (40:8). Yosef understands interpretation as a conscious process. How else could he interpret other people's dreams?

---

[20] If we continue to think cinematically, perhaps the camera pulls back further, revealing that the angel is also a projection.

Note that while Yosef tells his dreams to his brothers and father, he emphatically does not ask for help understanding them. Yaakov's outburst "*Is it really so that I, and your mother, and your brothers, will come to prostrate ourselves before you*?!" does not shake him. (Unlike Yaakov, Yosef and his brothers all understand that the moon is Leah. But the brothers also realize that the dreams are progressing. With apologies to lyricist Tim Rice, Joseph is a sheave, but he is not a star. The sun and moon and stars bow to him directly. That's why the celestial dream makes the brothers hate Yosef more.) Even in prison, Yosef remains confident that he understands his own dreams.

Chazal depict the "baker" and "butler" as somewhere in between Yosef and Yaakov. Pharaoh's servants know what their dreams are about, but not what they mean. The result is that they lose all agency; their dreams come to mean what Yosef says they do. (The "butler" may realize that the dream said nothing about showing gratitude to the interpreter, and therefore decides to bide his time before mentioning Yosef in the royal court.)

Finally, we come to Pharaoh. Unlike his underlings, he retains the agency to reject interpretations he dislikes, whether or not they accord well with the "text" of his dream.

Why does Pharaoh need an outside interpreter, when Yosef does not? My tentative suggestion is that Yosef wants to make his dreams come true, while Pharaoh wants to prevent his dreams from coming true. Yosef is inspired and energized by his dreams; Pharaoh is terrified and depressed by his.

No one dreams about anything but their own future. Pharaoh fully identifies himself with Egypt. Dreams about national Egyptian bounties and famines are therefore about him. But he redeems this egoism by maintaining that identification in the face of disaster. He seeks an interpretation that will save the nation rather than one that will enable him to avoid sharing its fate.

Yosef realizes that what Pharaoh needs is not an interpretation but an attitude. 'Of course that's what the dream means – but who says it's inevitable? My dreams won't happen unless I do something, and his dreams will happen unless he does something. Maybe it's G-d's will that my needs and his coincide.'

So Yosef tells Pharaoh that G-d sent him this dream as a warning and spur to action. As with the "butler", nothing in the dream means "*You must appoint a man of discernment and wisdom and place him over Egypt*", let alone identifies Yosef as that man. But Pharaoh realizes, as Yosef certainly intended, that no one else in the court had even considered the possibility that something productive could be done.

Moreover, no one else had the guts to provide a self-refuting interpretation. It's clear from the outset that if Yosef's policy is correct, his prediction will be proven incorrect. Just as the "butler" had no need to show gratitude to Yosef, because his reappointment might have happened anyway, Pharaoh will have no need to acknowledge that a famine would have happened absent Yosef's policy. This is the tack his successor takes in "not knowing Yosef".[21]

Yosef is often presented as the model successful Diaspora Jew. I always push back hard against this presentation on the ground that Yosef's policy leads us into centuries of slavery, which most plausibly is measure-for-measure retribution for his enslavement of the Egyptians to Pharaoh. Yosef makes the mistake of accepting the premise of Pharaoh's dream, that his interests and Egypt's are identical. Even a genuinely great Pharaoh's worldview is terribly distorted. (Deborah argues that Pharaoh's treatment of the "butler" and "baker" suggest that "great" is too generous.)

I recently read the autobiography of Bernard Baruch, once commonly presented as the model successful America Jew. It immediately put me in mind of Yosef. Baruch's life-story casts new light on the implications of Yosef for American Jews.

President Wilson desperately wanted to keep America out of World War I. Baruch was one of those who urged the necessity of preparing for war regardless. In 1915, in his first meeting with Wilson, he presented a

---

[21] Also: Nothing about Pharaoh's dream, or Yosef's initial interpretation, says anything about using the potential famine to turn Egypt into an absolutist monarchy in which the state owns all the land. I wonder how this Pharaoh would have reacted had Yosef included that at the start.

plan for a commission, headed by one wise and understanding man and reporting only to the president, that would have complete authority over the production and pricing of all militarily necessary materials within the United States and its allies.

Wilson finally asked for a declaration of war on April 2, 1917. By early 1918, he was convinced that Baruch had been correct. Even though Baruch had no administrative experience, Wilson called him to the White House and said: "After G-d has shown you all this, there is no one as wise and understanding as you", handed him the Presidential Seal, and appointed him to the job. Baruch thus went out to the land with unprecedented power. There were those who called him dictator. (He had particular trouble with Henry Ford, who refused to believe that there wasn't enough steel available to keep making both cars and tanks.) I'm fictionalizing the details, but you get the idea that Baruch was Joseph. And you've probably guessed from his name that Baruch was Jewish.

There is much to discuss about the content of Baruch's Jewish identity, and what it might help us understand about American Jewishness. But my interest here is that he never considered extending the powers of the War Industrial Board into peacetime. He conceptualized wartime economics as an emergency exception because the small sample-size meant that the market could not be trusted to properly regulate supply and demand.

Perhaps that was because Wilson's dream was peace, and Baruch himself had achieved great wealth as a young man and found it unsatisfying. (What drove Yosef's life once his family had bowed to him?) It's not only that dreams don't inevitably come true, but also that we are responsible for choosing our dreams, or at least which dreams matter to us. What is American Orthodoxy dreaming of?

Our horror at the massacre can't be sincere until we explain what should have happened instead.

Chapter 35

JUSTICE AND DINAH:
THE APPROACH OF RAV DOVID TZVI HOFFMAN,
AND ITS DISCONTENTS

The rape of Dinah and the massacre of Shekhem separately outrage us. Yet these reactions of horror are in tension. For our horror at the massacre to be sincere without diminishing our horror at the rape, we need to explain what should have happened instead. We need a specific response to the brothers' question: "*Should we allow him to treat our sister as a harlot?*"

The Torah here makes sure that we relate to sinners as more than the sum of their sins. Shekhem is a rapist, but one who seeks to make things right, as best he can within his own frame of moral reference. The brothers lie and murder and loot, but not without cause. The apparently least sympathetic character is Yaakov, who fails to deter or restrain evil, or to assume responsibility; and the apparently shallowest character is Dinah.

The Torah also eschews explicit evaluations of characters or actions. The characters evaluate each other, but we decide which evaluations to accept. Interpretations therefore necessarily depend on and reveal the interpreter's moral stances, the interpreter's understanding of the author's moral stances, or both. Interpreters with profound moral commitments and full confidence in the morality of the text and its Author will necessarily seek ways to square the text's commitments with their own. Where our moral commitments differ from theirs, we will likely find their interpretations forced or disingenuous, as they would find ours.

My goal this week is to clearly present and unflinchingly evaluate the interpretations of the great 20th century scholar Rabbi Dovid Tzvi Hoffman.

1.

Rabbi Hoffman begins by wondering why Dinah as a person is absent from the story. (As with Yosef and his brothers, she is transformed from subject to object by another's gaze. ADK) He responds that Dinah was likely a child of perhaps 8 or 9 – Shekhem speaks of her to his father (34:4) as *hayaldah hazot* = *that girl-child* – and therefore no one considered her opinions relevant.

I'm not convinced that this significantly mitigates the moral problem. Moreover, the narrator refers to her in 34:3 as a *naarah*, which suggests (as Rabbi Hoffman also acknowledges) that *yaldah* may be a term of affection, like the modern "baby".

2.

Rabbi Hoffman notes that the verbs (34:2) describing Shekhem's taking of Dinah - *vayishkav otah vayeaneha* are inverted in 2 Samuel 13:14's description of Amnon's rape of Tamar. He then notes that Avot 5:16 uses Amnon's love for Tamar as the paradigm of *ahavah hateluyah badavar*, conditional love, which the Mishnah asserts does not endure, as evidenced by Amnon's love for Tamar turning into greater hatred immediately after the rape. By contrast, Shekhem's emotional attachment and love come after the rape, and his love endures. Rabbi Hoffman even understands Shekhem "speaking to the heart of the lass" (34:3) as appeasement – perhaps even apology? rather than seduction.

Does Rabbi Hoffman mean to imply that Shekhem's love was genuine and unconditional? How should that effect our evaluation if it wasn't reciprocated by Dinah? If Dinah did eventually reciprocate, but while still in captivity, should we view her as suffering from "Stockholm syndrome" and therefore disregard her agency, or would that be abusing her further?

3.

Rabbi Hoffman notes that 34:5 reports that Yaakov heard of these events but did not directly respond. He defends Yaakov against the charge of indifference by citing Josephus' position that Yaakov actively sent for his sons, and by claiming that brothers customarily had a primary right of response in such matters. He draws an analogy to Lavan's active involvement in Rivkah's betrothal to Yitzchak (24:50).

This defense contradicts Rashi, who presents Lavan as wickedly usurping his father's role. Halakhah also clearly gives father's primary authority over minor daughters, with brothers playing a formal (and *derabanan*) role only if the father dies. Finally, Josephus' report notwithstanding, it seems to me more likely in the text that Yaakov passively waited for the brothers to appear, or assumed they were already on their way.

4.

Rabbi Hoffman contends that 34:7 contains two separable censures of Shekhem's act. First *nevalah asah b'Yisroel*, meaning that Yaakov's family morals were outraged. Second, *vekhen lo yeiaseh* – the rape of unattached women was forbidden by Canaanite law and morality as well (even though it is not obviously forbidden by the Seven Noachide Laws), and therefore, Shekhem's action threatened a total sociomoral breakdown. Rabbi Hoffman contends that this threat provides an element of justification for the brothers' subsequent actions.

However, he also notes that Shekhem is careful not to mention the rape when speaking to his townsmen. This suggests that they were also horrified by his actions, or would have been had they known of them. While Shekhem is described shortly after the rape (34:19) as "honored above all his father's house", perhaps that was only because of the cover-up. Shekhem and his father Chamor also make no open mention of the rape when speaking with Dinah's family (although Rabbi Hoffman suggests that 34:11 may contain a veiled apology).

Perhaps the townsmen knew only that a young woman had appeared in the camp. This might undermine any justification for broad-based retaliation.

Rabbi Hoffman notes that Chamor and Shekhem present the issue of circumcision as a matter of public good, and ongoing assimilation, without reference to Dinah at all. However, it seems to me that the willingness of Shekhem to pay any financial price, and the willingness of all the males of the city to undergo circumcision, suggest a consciousness of guilt. Perhaps everyone was trying to restore Shekhem's honor.

The question then is whether consciousness of guilt is a mitigating or aggravating factor, and how severely we regard their frantic desire to make everything right rather than punish the guilty. Here I wonder what Dinah was saying. But it seems no one paid attention to her.

5.

Rabbi Hoffman disappointingly draws no connection between 33:20: *Yaakov came shalem to Shekhem* and the statement of Chamor and Shekhem to the men of their city that *These men are shalem with us.* I think the connection is obvious but am not sure what it conveys.

6.

Rabbi Hoffman argues that the shifting epithets for the people of the city – *anshei ir, baei shaar, and yotz'ei shaar* - are interchangeable variants of one underlying phrase. This places him squarely in the tradition of Rashbam, whereas I am generally an antidisomnisignificantarian.

7.

Rabbi Hoffman follows Ramban in suggesting that Yaakov and his sons other than Shimon and Levi assumed that the demand for circumcision would be rejected. Even if it were accepted, they planned only to remove Dinah while the Shekhemites were incapacitated. Shimon and Levi independently planned the revenge massacre, and thus earned Yaakov's anger.

Rabbi Hoffman contends that the Torah sides with Yaakov. But he cannot refrain from defending Shimon and Levi.

"We can therefore explain this action as resulting from the disgust of the two brothers, a deep and burning disgust, to a point that did not allow them to consider how this action would bring them and their entire family into grave danger. They saw a terrible injury to the honor of their father's house and preferred death to humiliation. In such circumstances a person is not capable of rational thought. Anger pushes him to do deeds for which he is almost not responsible. It is this anger that Yaakov curses on his deathbed. The Torah expresses its verdict via Yaakov's verdict. Nonetheless, we can perceive in this verdict the ethical height of those judged".

Thank G-d for the "almost"!

8.

Rabbi Hoffman distinguishes (following Pseudo-Yonatan) between Shimon and Levi, who kill all the (convalescing) males and then take Dinah away, and the brothers who follow in their wake.

"Because they had defiled their sister. All the inhabitants of Shekhem were considered guilty, not only because not even one voice was raised against the wrong, but also because they had agreed to the circumcision in order to take into their hands later the property of Yaakov's family. They saw themselves as justified by what was done to Dinah . . . They did not kill anyone defenseless, but rather took them with them as spoil".

The Torah thus emphasizes that the other brothers had no part in the massacre. I wonder whether that is a sufficient explanation of why Yaakov does not condemn them.

9.

Rabbi Hoffman notes that Yaakov's anger at Shimon and Levi mentions only the danger they have brought upon the family, not the massacre. He argues that Shimon and Levi were too enraged to hear any moral criticism. The only hope was for the practical critique to make them realize how out-of-control they were. When they respond "death before dishonor", Yaakov has nothing left to say to them:

"If the lives of their parents and brothers were not important in their eyes, how could one speak to their hearts about the lives of those sinners? It is very likely that Yaakov already cursed their anger in his heart, but he did not see fit to express his feeling in words at that point, but rather preserved the matter until his death".

Perhaps Yaakov was scared of Shimon and Levi. But in this reading Yaakov never condemns the other brothers, which suggests that he condones their actions.

10.
Overall:
Rabbi Hoffman recognizes and addresses the depersonalization of Dinah, although his response to the implicit feminist critique comes at the cost of denying children any agency. He recognizes the wrong of the massacre but yet tries to mitigate it, running the risk of understanding too much and therefore forgiving too much. His failure to condemn the actions of the second wave of brothers is textually reasonable but disappointed me.

A traditional reading cannot leave the founding fathers of our tribes utterly without virtue, and at least Levi's anger is ultimately redeemed by his descendants' reaction to the Golden Calf (and yet they are given no contiguous land in Israel, lest they unite.) Rabbi Hoffman is noticeably modern in the issues he addresses, and in his disinterest in framing the conversation around technical Noahide law rather than universal morality. Yet I am left wanting more agency for Dinah, and a more robust accounting for the dead of Shekhem.

Chapter 36

WHAT HAPPENED TO YOSEF'S OTHER CHILDREN?

Feeling intimations of mortality, Yaakov summons his son, the viceroy Yosef, and begs him (Bereishis 47:29):

אל נא תקברני במצרים

Please do not bury me in Egypt.

Yaakov came down to Egypt with every intention and expectation of dying there. He did not try to leave during his lifetime. So why was it so important to him to not be buried there?

Note that his request begins with and focuses on being removed from Egypt. Burial in the ancestral gravesite is secondary, and the Land of Israel is not mentioned at all.

I suggest that Yaakov is not so much expressing his own needs as trying to make a point to Yosef.

Yaakov and Yosef next meet when Yaakov becomes mortally ill. This time the conversation is all about the Land: (48:4-7)

וַיֹּאמֶר אֵלַי

הִנְנִי מַפְרְךָ וְהִרְבִּיתִךָ וּנְתַתִּיךָ לִקְהַל עַמִּים

וְנָתַתִּי אֶת־הָאָרֶץ הַזֹּאת לְזַרְעֲךָ אַחֲרֶיךָ אֲחֻזַּת עוֹלָם:

וְעַתָּה

שְׁנֵי־בָנֶיךָ הַנּוֹלָדִים לְךָ בְּאֶרֶץ מִצְרַיִם

עַד־בֹּאִי אֵלֶיךָ מִצְרַיְמָה –

לִי־הֵם

אֶפְרַיִם וּמְנַשֶּׁה - כִּרְאוּבֵן וְשִׁמְעוֹן יִהְיוּ־לִי:

וּמוֹלַדְתְּךָ אֲשֶׁר־הוֹלַדְתָּ אַחֲרֵיהֶם –

לְךָ יִהְיוּ

עַל שֵׁם אֲחֵיהֶם יִקָּרְאוּ בְּנַחֲלָתָם:

וַאֲנִי

בְּבֹאִי מִפַּדָּן מֵתָה עָלַי רָחֵל

בְּאֶרֶץ כְּנַעַן בַּדֶּרֶךְ בְּעוֹד כִּבְרַת־אֶרֶץ לָבֹא אֶפְרָתָה

וָאֶקְבְּרֶהָ שָּׁם בְּדֶרֶךְ אֶפְרָת הִוא בֵּית לָחֶם:

(G-d) said to me:
Behold I am making you fruitful and I will multiply you
and I will place you as a congregation of nations
and I will give this land to your seed after you as a permanent holding.
Now
your two sons, who were born to you in the Land of Egypt,
until I came to you to Egypt –
they are mine;
Ephraim and Menasheh will be for me like Reuven and Shim'on
but those you sired, whom you sired after them –
they will be yours
they will be called by their brothers' name in their homestead.
And I –
when I was coming from Padan, Rachel died on me
in the Land of Canaan on the way, while we were still far from Efrat,
so I buried her there on the way to Efrat, which is Beit Lechem.

Something seems to be off here. Efraim and Menashe, who were born before Yaakov arrived and restored the family connection to Canaan, receive an independent share of the land. Later sons, who were raised with the connection to Canaan assumed, do not. Why?

I suggest that the answer lies in the point that Yaakov tried to make to Yosef at their previous meeting. To elucidate that point, we'll first discuss a more recent Egyptian experience, and then Rav Yehudah Herzl Henkin z"l's analysis of Yaakov's treatment of Yosef's sons.

Until the 19th century, Christians in Ottoman Egypt were required to wear special attire and pay special taxes as a disfavored minority. The Egyptian nationalism that arose under the rule of Muhammad Ali Pasha (1805-1848) fostered a new Egyptian identity that included Coptic Christians. Members of the Coptic economic elite now attained political and social prominence. One example was Boutros Ghali, who became prime minister (under King Fuad) in 1908 and served until being assassinated in 1910.

On Boutros Ghali's deathbed, he called in his grandson Boutros Boutros-Ghali (later Egyptian Foreign Minister under President Anwar Sadat, and UN Secretary General) and made him swear to bury him in Paris. The parallel to Yosef – the model representative of an alien minority who becomes second-in-command, only to recognize at the last moment that he is not really home – seems too perfect to be true.

Which it is – I invented that scene to draw out the parallel. But the grandson's memoir Egypt's Road to Jerusalem does contain a passage that reminds me very much of Yaakov's earlier conversation with Yosef:

We left for Alexandria aboard a special train that had belonged to King Fuad. very year at the start of the summer season the king had taken this train from Cairo to Alexandria, accompanied by all his cabinet members, making Alexandria for three months the second capital of Egypt. Then in September, they would return via the same train, with the same ceremony, to Cairo. For generations, every member of the Egyptian oligarchy had to own a second residence in Alexandria. As a boy, I was obsessed by such social niceties and humiliated because my family did not own a second residence in Alexandria but only rented a villa there. Every time I asked my father to buy a villa, he would ask me whether I preferred our second residence to be in Alexandria or in Europe. I would always reply "Europe!" "Then, do you see why we have no Alexandria villa?" my father would ask.

I wonder where his father chose to be buried. Boutros Boutros-Ghali nominally lived in Egypt throughout his life, occupying prominent positions but with no real authority. (I suspect that was Yosef's role toward the end of his life.) He spent as much time as he could in Europe.

Rav Yehuda Herzl Henkin z"l's essay on Vayechi[22] recognizes the complex situation facing children of elites who are nonetheless "others" in the society that gives them power. His starting question is: Why does Yaakov grant Tribe status to Yosef's sons who grew up without his influence, and deny it to those he knew from the cradle? Shouldn't it be the other way around?

Yosef certainly had sons aside from Efraim and Menasheh, as in Yaakov's statement *"but your progeny whom you sired after them..."*

[22] Shu"t Bnei Banim vol. 4, p. 128, available on Hebrew Books and Sefaria; translated in New Interpretations on the Parsha, but the translation below is my own)

(48:6). Even according to Rashi's opinion that this statement was made in future tense = 'if you sire more,' as Onkelos had translated, we must say that in the end such sons were born. Otherwise, why would the Torah tell us of things that Yaakov said which were purely theoretical?

At first glance, the mystery is deep. There is not mention of additional sons of Yosef anywhere else in Scripture, nor in texts of Chazal. They do not appear in Parshat Bamidbar in the lists of the Children of Israel who exited Egypt, so it seems that they did not exit. They assimilated, remained in Egypt, and their traces were lost.

On this basis we can understand Yaakov's words:

Now, your two sons that were born to you in the Land of Mitzrayim ere I came to you to Mitzrayim –
they are mine.
Efraim and Menasheh, like Reuven and Shimon, will be mine.
But your progeny whom you sired after them –
they will be yours;
they will be called under their brother's names in their homesteads."

Yaakov and his sons had portable wealth: silver and gold, flocks and cattle and camels. Just as they brought this wealth into Egypt, they would be able to bring it out. But Yosef, the one with authority over the land, had fields and vineyards, houses and palaces full of all goods – immobile possessions that could not be transported.

So this is what Yaakov meant by saying: "*Now, your two sons that were born to you in the Land of Mitzrayim ere I came to you to Mitzrayim – they are mine. Efraim and Menasheh, like Reuven and Shimon, will be mine.*" Efraim and Menasheh will be like the son of Yaakov for all purposes, and they will share in the estate of their grandfather equally with Reuven, Shimon, and their father's other brothers, whereas the wealth of Yosef will be inherited by Yosef's other sons and not by Efraim and Menasheh. This is the meaning of "*they will be called under their brother's names in their homesteads*": "called under X's name" means that one person takes another's place as heir, as in Devarim 25:6: "*So the first-born to whom she subsequently gives birth will stand up under the name of his dead brother*" which is speaking about inheritance. Yaakov was concerned that if Ephraim and Menasheh would inherit their father, they would take possession of his wealth, and when the day of redemption came – they would not want to leave. This is what Yaakov sought to prevent in every way.

All the above (parshanut) was revealed in our beit midrash. It remains to ask: Why did Yaakov foresee that the remaining sons of Yosef would melt (into Egyptian society), and therefore he focused on saving Efraim and Menasheh alone? Really it should be the reverse: If Efraim and Menasheh, who were born and reached the age of educability while Yosef was by himself in Egypt, before the arrival of Yaakov and his brothers, nonetheless remained faithful to Israel and his Torah, then all the more so their younger brothers, who were born when they already had a grandfather in Egypt, (should have remained faithful)!

But it seems to me that this is not astounding, and there are several explanations for the matter:

1)
When Yosef was by himself in Egypt, he took pains to educate Efraim and Menasheh in the heritage of his father's household, because who other than him would do it? But after his family reached Egypt, he did not devote himself to the education of his other sons to the same extent, but rather relied on the family influence. However, this influence was not effective, because Yosef and his sons lived in Egypt's capital, the place of the king and officers, and not with Yaakov and his sons in the Land of Goshen.

2)
Before his father and brothers arrived, Yosef felt alone and solitary in Egypt, as emerges from the names by which he called his two sons. He transmitted this feeling of alienation to Efraim and Menasheh, and this was effective in enabling them to avoid blending into Egypt. However, after Yaakov's household arrived, Yosef felt expansive and relaxed in Egypt, and his younger sons felt even more this way, and therefore they blended in, and ultimately melted.

3)

What is astounding is not that Yosef's other sons assimilated, since they were members of the elite in Egypt. The astounding thing is that Efraim and Menasheh did not melt also. However, Efraim and Menasheh saw and experienced the spiritual whirlwind that passed over their father when Yosef made himself known to his brothers and when Yaakov came to him in Egypt. These experiences left a deep impression in their souls and served as a shield against assimilation, which was lacking for Yosef's other sons.

The fundamental question Rav Henkin raises is whether we can reasonably expect Orthodox children in America to become authentic Jewish leaders. This is powerful stuff from a posek so vital to our community's development. We owe it a full hearing whether or not we end up agreeing. Note that Rav Henkin himself made Aliyah in 1972.

Rav Henkin's third answer is that Yosef's two oldest children observed and experienced how deeply his identity was affected by Yaakov's arrival. Yosef became a baal teshuvah, and his family became baalei teshuvah with him. But later children would grow up knowing firsthand only the restrictions generated by those experiences. They would experience these restrictions as externally imposed rather than as autonomously assumed, and therefore would not find them meaningful. There are ways to avoid this trap. Yaakov knew Yosef too well to believe that he would adopt them.

Rav Henkin's second answer is that Yaakov's arrival made Egypt into 'home' for his family. This sounds like a charedi critique of Modern Orthodoxy, but historical context inverts the parallel. The most likely parallel to Yaakov's arrival in Egypt is the post WWII arrival of European Torah greats in America. The main worry is not assimilation of individuals, but assimilation of the community as a whole. Yosef's later children would superficially maintain their Jewish identity and Orthodox practice, but their values and their prejudices would become fundamentally Egyptian.

Rav Henkin's first answer is the most subtle and yet perhaps the most directly challenging. Yosef was a successful father when fully engaged, but it's also true that the village matters. You just have to make sure it's the right village.

Maybe the village that matters most is not where you live, which can be dictated by duty or economic necessity, but where you would **choose** to be, and with whom. Do you buy in Alexandria and rent in Paris, or buy in Paris and rent in Alexandria? In other words: Are you in Alexandria because you must be, or because your fundamental identity and desires are those of a royal hanger-on? Yosef's later children spent vacations in Goshen out of duty and necessity, but lived in Cairo by choice.

Rav Henkin's analogy between America and Egypt challenges to make us think about where we live. But it applies even more to how we spend time.

Chapter 37

A REVIEW OF THE LIFE OF MOSES BY JORGE LUIS BORGES

"The night I was bar mitzvah", the Mistakener Ilui often told his students, "an angel – or maybe a demon - came to me in a dream and offered me a choice of yeshivas. I could either go to a place where I already understood everything, or to a place where I would understand nothing. I chose the first; you chose the second. I envy you." None of the students understood what he was saying. But they wrote the story down anyway. I have read the story many times now, and sometimes I think I understand him.

A biography of my grandfather's rebbe, Rav Meir Shapiro ("the Lubliner"), contains a chapter titled "From Ilui to Gaon". I'm sure the author had no idea how devastating the Mistakener would find it. Most yeshiva prodigies happily carry the label "ilui" into old age without any sense that they could have become something more, and they are almost always correct. But the Mistakener was unhappy still being an ilui, and he was right to be unhappy.

I met him once, at a joyous occasion – his student's daughter was marrying my student. Of course I seized the opportunity to schmooze in learning with a famous ilui. The parshah was Ki Sisa, and like every other Modern Orthodox rabbi, I was preparing a shiur about the aggadeta on Menachot 29b, Mosheh Rabbeinu time-travelling to Rabbi Akiva's classroom. So I asked him if he had any *chiddushim* about it. He said: "I have no chiddushim. But some of what I find obvious might be new to you, so I'm happy to schmooze". We talked for about fifteen minutes before he had to go. As soon as he left, I tried desperately to write everything down before it went out of my head. Here are some of my notes:

Said Rav Yehudah said Rav:
At the time that Mosheh Rabbeinu went on High, he found The Holy Blessed One sitting tying crowns to the letters. He said to him:
"Master of the universe, who is meakev al yadkha?"

The word *meakev* literally means to prevent, to delay. The phrase *meakev al yad* refers specifically to placing a legal restraint on someone else's authority, for example by enforcing the conditions of a lease. What does this have to do with tying crowns on letters?

Bava Basra 16a:
Said Rava:
Iyov tried to exempt the entire universe from Judgment. He said before Him:
Master of the universe, You created the ox with split hooves, and You created the donkey with sealed hooves; You created Gan Eden, and You created GeiHinom; You created the righteous, and You created the wicked: who is meakev al Yadkha?

Bereshis Rabba 49:
Said R Yehudah:
(Avraham Avinu said to Hashem):
When You sought to judge Your world, You gave it into the hands of a duumvirate, as for example Remus and Romulus, that if one of them sought to do something, the other would be meakev al yado;
but You, because You (are "the judge of all the land" and therefore) have no one to be meakev al Yadkha, will You not do justice?!

Iyov argues that Hashem's absolute power should enable Him to avoid doing justice, while Avraham argues that His absolute power should not enable Him to avoid doing justice. This seems like a blatant contradiction.

But it isn't a contradiction at all. Iyov and Avraham both try to stop Hashem from punishing in a way they see as substantively unjust . Iyov protests Hashem's use of procedural justice – the forms of law, due process – to accomplish substantive injustice, because really He can only blame Himself for the existence of wickedness. Avraham protests the substantive injustice of punishing the righteous together with the wicked.

Iyov and Avraham both fail as defense attorneys. Iyov fails because his friends correctly answer that human beings have free will: "Hashem created the Evil Inclination, and He created Torah as its remedy". We don't know for certain why Avraham fails, but Hashem destroys Sodom despite his objection.

Avraham's argument is really dangerous and astonishing. Does he *chas veshalom* really want Hashem to appoint a co-Master of the universe?! What he means is that Hashem should allow the Attributes of Justice/*Din* and Mercy to balance each other in His relationship with the universe, and he thought that Sodom was being judged by pure *Din*. (He was wrong; under pure *Din*, Lot and his unmarried daughters would not have survived.) Similarly, Iyov was wrong to argue for a world without *Din* at all.

So tying the crowns onto the letters must be a question of *din* and *rachamim*.

Hashem replies to Mosheh that the crowns are necessary because Rabbi Akiva will learn mounds of laws from them. He takes Mosheh to Rabbi Akiva's *beis medrash*, where Mosheh understands nothing, and grows depressed, until Rabbi Akiva answers a student's question about the source of one law by saying that it is a tradition received by Mosheh from Sinai. Mosheh then turns to Hashem and asks: "You have such a man, and You give the Torah through me = *al yadi*?" Hashem replies: "Be silent! So it arose in thought before Me". Mosheh asks to see Rabbi Akiva's reward, and is shown his flayed flesh being weighed in the marketplace. He protests to Hashem: "This is Torah, and this is its reward?!" Hashem replies again: "Be silent! So it arose in thought before Me".

The phrase "arose in thought" is famously cited by Rashi in his explanation of why the first narrative of Creation in Bereishis refers to Hashem as Elo-him, while the second narrative uses the compound Hashem Elo-him.

It initially arose in thought to create it with the attribute of Din exclusively. He saw that the universe would not last, so he prioritized the attribute of Din and partnered it with that of Mercy.

Maharal in Gur Aryeh explains that according to Rashi, Hashem would still prefer a world of pure Din, if it could only last, and therefore "Fortunate is the person who can withstand the Attribute of Din, and has no need for Mercy." Rav Dessler makes the connection to Rabbi Akiva: the reward for his Torah was the opportunity to live, however briefly and painfully, in the world of pure Din.

Rabbi Akiva himself understood this. That's why we read on Berakhot 61b that he greeted martyrdom as an opportunity to fulfill "*You must love Hashem with all heart, wealth, and nefesh* – meaning even if He takes your *nefesh*." But we also read there that the angels reacted by asking Hashem: "This is Torah and this is its reward?!" The angels did not understand that the reality of punishment was an essential part of Rabbi Akiva's reward.

The author of this aggadeta wants to make sure that we understand the connection. The dramatic climax of the story in Berakhot is Rabbi Akiva reciting the Shma while being tortured, and "his *neshomoh* departed at the word *echad*". Here, Hashem tells Mosheh Rabbeinu about Rabbi Akiva by saying "אחד יש שעתיד להיות בסוף כמה דורות אדם", "there is an *echad* person who will be after many generations". Moreover, it seems that Mosheh arrives in Rabbi Akiva's classroom on the day that he teaches this topic.

כיון שהגיע לדבר אחד, אמרו לו תלמידיו: רבי, מנין לך?
אמר להן: הלכה למשה מסיני.
When he reached the matter of echad, his students said to him:
Rebbe, what is your source for this?
He said to them: It is a tradition of Mosheh from Sinai.

But Mosheh Rabbeinu did not understand what Rabbi Akiva was talking about. He asks Hashem the same question as the angels: "This is Torah, and this is its reward?!" Mosheh Rabbeinu did not understand that Rabbi Akiva was living and dying in fulfillment of his own interpretation of Torah.

It further seems that Hashem intends Mosheh Rabbeinu to misunderstand, because Hashem shows him only the grotesquerie of Rabbi Akiva's flesh being weighed in the marketplace, and not the scene of total faith and commitment that preceded it. But then why does Hashem answer Mosheh Rabbeinu's question at all?

The answer is that this conversation takes place **before** Hashem gives Mosheh Rabbeinu the Torah – it seems that Hashem can't give it until the crowns are tied on. We also need to realize that this *aggadeta* is based on Shemot 31:8:

ויתן אל משה ככלתו לדבר אתו בהר סיני שני לחת

He gave to Mosheh when He finished speaking with him on Har Sinai two tablets

Hashem could not give Mosheh the Torah **until He finished speaking with him**. The conversation is what tied the crowns on.

God tells Mosheh that Rabbi Akiva will derive heaps of laws from the crowns. But that doesn't mean that anyone else will understand how the crowns lead to the laws. As far as everyone else is concerned, Rabbi Akiva's laws can only be justified as "a tradition of Mosheh from Sinai". Which they are – the Torah that Mosheh receives and transmits has the crowns attached, and the crowns are real, and they mean what Rabbi Akiva says they do.

But the letters without the crowns would not mean the same thing. The Torah's meaning changes when the conversation between Hashem and Mosheh Rabbeinu ties the crowns on.

The Torah represents the universe. To understand the universe G-d created, we need to understand why G-d originally thought of creating a different universe, one with only Din. To receive the Torah, Mosheh Rabbeinu needed to understand this *hava amina*. Torah makes no sense if mercy is always better than justice, if having to account to G-d for our lives is a bug rather than a feature. The crowns on the letters represent that *hava amina*.

Empathy with Hashem's *hava amina* is dangerous. Torah leaders must never regard someone else's suffering with equanimity, even if that suffering can be seen as an expression of justice. Rabbi Akiva would not have said Shma the same way at someone else's martyrdom. To receive the Torah, Mosheh Rabbeinu needed to maintain belief in the necessity of mercy, to the point of regarding a failure to show mercy as injustice. "Shall the Judge of all the land not do justice?!"

That's what I have in my notes. The last thing he said to me I didn't have to write down. It carried such emotional power that could never forget it. He said that it was the experience of Rabbi Akiva's classroom that turned Mosheh Rabbeinu from an ilui into a gaon.

(Note: The Mistakener Ilui is a purely fictional character. Some of the connections and readings in this essay were drawn from or inspired by Rav Ari Kahn's title essay in The Crowns on the Letters, *which I encourage you to read.)*

Think of Rachav facing the spies as parallel to Rabban Yochanan ben Zakkai facing Vespasian

Chapter 38

A TALE OF TWO CITIES

Rabbi Norman Lamm z"l liked to say that "Halakhah is a floor, not a ceiling"[23]. His point was that halakhah does not constitute the entirety of Jewish and human obligation. Once astonishingly prevalent in Yeshiva University circles, that idea is rarely heard today except in the context of Rav Aharon Lichtenstein's inverted claim that all Jewish and human obligations, however derived, are halakhah.

Ramban wrote that Halakhah is not a solid floor. Because a legal system cannot account for all the details of life, one can be a *naval birshut haTorah* = a disgusting person acting under the authority of Halakhah, and fall through into spiritual cellars or dungeons.

Architectural metaphors generally carry connotations of fixedness and objectivity. Floor and ceiling remain the same distance from each other, and for every person. We might need more dynamic analogies to express the ways in which human beings can subjectively alter the relationship between halakhic and other obligations.

The simplest method is to take an oath that has halakhic force. An oath of *nezirut*, for instance. We can say that the additional prohibitions against consuming alcohol and becoming *tamei* raise the floor, and also lower certain ceilings; for example, a *nazir* cannot participate in a *chevra kadisha*. Do *nazirs* and *kohanim* really live within a more constricted range of spiritual possibilities? Imagining the *nazir* as having more elbowroom but less headroom doesn't seem to really capture the experience.

However, I think this framing can usefully force us to consider whether the reverse case exists. Can human decisions lower halakhic floors, and raise spiritual ceilings? How should we evaluate decisions

---

[23] Others cite the same phrase from Rabbi Walter Wurzburger in the name of Rabbi Yosef Dov Soloveitchik, but my recollection is of Rabbi Lamm saying it without attributing it to someone else.

that do both simultaneously? Can our commitments affect other people's spiritual range?

One case that interests me is the commitment that the spies make to Rachav HaZonah in Yericho. Their dialogue takes place in Yehoshua 2:9-14, **after** she has already hidden them and misdirected the authorities searching for them.

וַתֹּאמֶר אֶל־הָאֲנָשִׁים:
"יָדַעְתִּי
כִּי־נָתַן יְקֹוָק לָכֶם אֶת־הָאָרֶץ
וְכִי־נָפְלָה אֵימַתְכֶם עָלֵינוּ
וְכִי נָמֹגוּ כָּל־יֹשְׁבֵי הָאָרֶץ מִפְּנֵיכֶם.
כִּי שָׁמַעְנוּ
אֵת אֲשֶׁר־הוֹבִישׁ יְקֹוָק אֶת־מֵי יַם־סוּף מִפְּנֵיכֶם בְּצֵאתְכֶם מִמִּצְרָיִם
וַאֲשֶׁר עֲשִׂיתֶם לִשְׁנֵי מַלְכֵי הָאֱמֹרִי אֲשֶׁר בְּעֵבֶר הַיַּרְדֵּן
לְסִיחֹן וּלְעוֹג אֲשֶׁר הֶחֱרַמְתֶּם אוֹתָם:
וַנִּשְׁמַע וַיִּמַּס לְבָבֵנוּ וְלֹא־קָמָה עוֹד רוּחַ בְּאִישׁ מִפְּנֵיכֶם
כִּי יְקֹוָק אֱ-לֹהֵיכֶם הוּא אֱ-לֹהִים בַּשָּׁמַיִם מִמַּעַל וְעַל־הָאָרֶץ מִתָּחַת:
וְעַתָּה
הִשָּׁבְעוּ־נָא לִי בַּיקֹוָק
כִּי־עָשִׂיתִי עִמָּכֶם חָסֶד
וַעֲשִׂיתֶם גַּם־אַתֶּם עִם־בֵּית אָבִי חֶסֶד
וּנְתַתֶּם לִי אוֹת אֱמֶת:
וְהַחֲיִתֶם אֶת־אָבִי וְאֶת־אִמִּי וְאֶת־אַחַי וְאֶת־אַחְיוֹתַי וְאֵת כָּל־אֲשֶׁר לָהֶם
וְהִצַּלְתֶּם אֶת־נַפְשֹׁתֵינוּ מִמָּוֶת."
וַיֹּאמְרוּ לָהּ הָאֲנָשִׁים:
"נַפְשֵׁנוּ תַחְתֵּיכֶם לָמוּת אִם לֹא תַגִּידוּ אֶת־דְּבָרֵנוּ זֶה
וְהָיָה בְּתֵת־יְקֹוָק לָנוּ אֶת־הָאָרֶץ
וְעָשִׂינוּ עִמָּךְ חֶסֶד וֶאֱמֶת.
She said to the men:
"I have come to know
that Hashem has given you the land
and that your terror has fallen upon us
and that all the inhabitants of the land tremble before you,
because we have heard that Hashem swept away the waters of
the Reed Sea from before you
and what you did to the two Kings of the Amorites across the
Yarden

to Sichon and Og, that you devastated them;
we heard, and our hearts melted away, and no man could any
longer sustain his spirit because of you
because Hashem your G-d, He is the God in the heavens above,
and on the land below.
Now -
swear to me, please, by Hashem
that/because I have done *chesed* to you
and you also will do *chesed* with my father's house
and you will give me a true sign,
You will give life to my father and my mother and my brothers
and my sisters and all who are theirs
and you will preserve our souls from death.
The men said to her:
"Our souls in your steads to death
if you do not tell of our matters
then it will be that when Hashem gives us the land
we will do *chesed* and *emet* with you.

Rachav's speech calls to mind the opening verses of Parshat Yitro, where Yitro similarly reports having heard all that G-d did for the Jews in Mitzrayim, and Az Yashir, which predicts the psychological impact she reports. Apparently the 39-year delay in the Jews' arrival has not diminished G-d's image of power, or else that image was revived by the total defeat inflicted on Sichon and Og.

What genre are we dealing with here? It's easy to read this as a conversion narrative, which is a standard way of understanding Yitro. Rachav recognizes that G-d is One above and below, and that G-d has a special relationship with the Jewish people, and so she asks to join them.

However, Rachav also asks for the lives of her biological family, and perhaps the lives of their loved ones as well. With apologies to Malbim, there is no basis in the text for saying that any of these would convert. Rachav is an excellent precedent for contemporary beit din practice, which recognizes not just the reality but the value of converts maintaining (healthy) emotional ties with their biological families. We saw last week as well that Yitro planned to return to his *eretz* and *moledet* (although possibly his leaving out *el beit avi* was significant, and also some commentaries assume that his motive for returning was to proselytize his family).

However, what gave the spies the authority to grant Rachav's request? Wasn't there a specific Divine command to spare no (unconverted) Canaanite? Note that Rachav says "please", and nothing in her language suggests an ultimatum. She makes the request only after lying about the spies to those searching for them, meaning after she has surrendered the power to expose them without risking herself. There is no quid pro quo here.

But Rachav does emphasize that saving her loved ones would be THE RIGHT THING TO DO. Radak notes that she described herself as having done *chesed* to them because they had as yet done nothing for her; a commentary that AlHatorah.org identifies only as "from the Sages of France" makes her appeal explicit:

וראוי לכם לעשות כן כי עשיתי עמכם חסד –
It is **fitting** for you to do so **because** I have done *chesed* with you

Abravanel understands Rachav as arguing that since she had saved two of them, they had a moral obligation to save that extended beyond her as a single individual. But that would seem to grant her only one relative. Ho'il Mosheh, by contrast, notes that the spies promise to do both *chesed* and *emet* for her; *emet* required them to reciprocate by saving her, but saving her family was an act of *chesed*, like G-d saving not only Lot but Lot's family from Sodom for the sake of Avraham. But what justified the spies to commit to a voluntary *chesed* in defiance of a Divine command? If such a *chesed* is legitimate, does it have any necessary limits?

Ralbag (=Gersonides) reads Rachav facing the spies as parallel to Rabban Yochanan ben Zakkai facing Vespasian before the Destruction of the Second Temple. She has their goodwill – but how far will that goodwill extend? Is her family (=Yavneh and its sages) the most she can save, or should she ask for her entire nation? If she asks for too much, she will probably lose everything. She reasons that her moral claim is on the spies as individuals, because the G-d of Israel can bring them victory whether or not their mission is successful, and therefore it would be utterly improper (פנים לא יאות להם בשום) for the spies to commit to permitting another large nation to remain in their land . So she makes the same decision as Rabban Yochanan, and likely also wonders for the rest of her life whether that decision beatified or damned her.

Ralbag's psychological reconstruction suggests that had Rachav felt she had a moral claim on the Jewish nation, she might well have asked for her entire people to be spared, and the spies might have acceded, if that could be done without impeding the conquest.

One might think that "leave no soul alive" (=לא תחיה כל נשמה) set the halakhic floor for the Conquest. But Rachav's active recognition of the legitimacy and inevitability of the Jewish return to Israel gave her the moral right to demand that the spies raise the halakhic floor by taking an oath to save her family.

The spies' oath raised the halakhic floor to the level of the moral floor. But it seems likely that Rachav's demand did not raise the moral floor – she merely enabled the spies to correctly perceive its level. They were halakhically obligated once they took the oath, but they were morally obligated to take the oath, In fact, they were obligated to take the oath even before made any demand, because without such an oath, halakhah was setting its ceiling below the moral floor.

The mass fast that Mordekhai arranged was both an impressive display of unity, and/or an impressive job of designing a political action that covered up disunity.

Chapter 39

MORDEKHAI'S POLITICS, AND OURS

Most years, we Jews use texts to teach ourselves about reality. For example, hundreds of edifying articles come out each Adar with titles like "Leadership Secrets of Haman the Agagite", or "How to Win Husbands and Influence Emperors". This year, I think everything should be turned upside down. We should use reality to teach ourselves about the megillah. In fact, we may need to assimilate what we've been taught by reality before we can learn from the megillah again.

Let's start where most such essays begin, with a discussion of whether Achashverosh was a wise or rather a foolish king. This argument often becomes a sort of latke-hamantaschen debate. Before the first drink, one side will point out the ridiculousness of legislating male domestic dominance, while the other will note the wisdom of cutting taxes; after the second or third drink, positions reverse, and so forth.

This year's reality taught me that there is no need to argue. The same ruler can be perceived both ways, on the basis of the same evidence, by different political factions and social groups.

This is not obvious. While presidents and their policies are often controversial, generally the disputes are about whether their decisions are principled or pandering, or about whether they are following the opinions of the correct group of experts. For the same ruler to be perceived simultaneously as either brilliant or mindless, calculating or random, happens less often (although it was also true of Reagan).

What if Megillat Esther was deliberately written to allow for both narratives? What if, by withdrawing His presence from the explicit narration, G-d turned Scripture into the ultimate work of impartial media, so that all political sides could trust His reporters?

232

This might mean that the Jews of the Persian Empire were also deeply split about whether Achashverosh was really on their side. Which makes Mordekhai and Esther's feat of arranging a bipartisan fast even more remarkable.

You may ask: How could the Jews of Shushan think that Achashverosh was on their side, when he had signed a decree authorizing genocide against them? The answer is that they knew all along that the initial genocide decree was a trick to get the anti-Semites (many of whom were also pedophiles) to reveal themselves, so they could be absolutely crushed.

Mordekhai and Esther found a way to argue for the fast *mimah nafshakh*: If the threat of genocide was real, then of course a fast was necessary; and if it was a trick, then it was essential not to tip the enemy off by acting relaxed.

Another possibility is that many Jews believed that Achashverosh was unaware of the planned genocide against them, and would stop it if he knew. So they supported the fast as a nonviolent public demonstration intended to get the king's attention.

This view of Achashverosh is in fact the position of Rabbi Yitzhak Shmuel Reggio, a student of ShaDaL (Rabbi S. D. Luzzatto), whose highly original commentary is now available on AlHatorah.org. He notes that Haman never mentions the name of his target nation in his pitch to Achashverosh, and that the genocidal decree is written in accordance with "everything that Haman commanded", likely with Achashverosh out of the room.

So the fast was on one level an impressive display of unity, and on another an impressive job of designing a political action that people could enthusiastically participate in together while strongly disagreeing with each other about why.

The Talmudic discussion (Megillah 12a) of Achashverosh's acumen focuses on a different detail. Chapter 1 tells us that Achashverosh first made a feast for his entire kingdom, and only afterward for the people in Shushan.

רב ושמואל;

חד אמר: מלך פיקח היה;
וחד אמר: מלך טיפש היה.
מאן דאמר מלך פיקח היה - שפיר עבד דקריב רחיקא ברישא,
דבני מאתיה, כל אימת דבעי - מפייס להו;
ומאן דאמר טפש היה - דאיבעי ליה לקרובי בני מאתיה ברישא,
דאי מרדו ביה הנך - הני הוו קיימי בהדיה.
Rav and Shmuel (disagreed):
One said: He was a clever king;
One said: He was a foolish king.
The one who said he was a clever king – he did well to first attract
those further away,
as the people of his city he could appease whenever he wanted;
The one who said he was a foolish king – he should have first brought
the people of his city close,
so that if the others revolted against him, they would stand with him.

The first side argues that to rule a genuinely multicultural empire, you need to build coalitions with ethnic groups aside from your own. Massive government feasts are a good start, but Achashverosh – being clever - realized that he also needed to make explicit gestures toward cultural autonomy, even if that meant entrenching misogyny. Hence "So that every man would reign in his house, and speak his ethnic tongue". In an identity-based body politic, the base's loyalty is deep, stubborn, and easily renewable.

The other side argued that the one must always first secure the base. It's true they won't turn against you regardless, but in key moments, turnout is crucial – you need the base to be hyper-enthusiastic, not sullenly loyal.

Eisenstein's Otzar HaMidrashim cites a darker and more authoritarian formulation of the dispute:

יש מי שאומר שחכם היה
שעשה משתה בראשונה לכל אנשי המדינות הרחוקות
מפני שאנשי עירו לא יוכלו למרוד בו,
מפני שהיה מצוי עמהם תמיד והם ברשותו,
לכן הקדים אנשי המדינות הרחוקות;
ויש מי שאמר: מלך טפש היה
לפי שהיה צריך לכבד אנשי עירו בתחלה,

ובהם יוכל לכוף אנשי המדינות האחרות,
ולא עשה כהוגן

One says that he was wise
in that he made the banquet first for all the people of the distant
provinces
because the people of his city would not be able to rebel against him,
because he is constantly among them and they are in his direct
authority.
That's why he prioritized the men of distant provinces.
But one says that he was a foolish king
because he needed to honor the people of his city first,
and with them he could subdue all the men of the other provinces,
so his policy was incorrect.

In this version, the loyalty of the base is grounded in fear of retaliation, not shared identity, and the empire is conquered in the first place by a small band of loyalists.

Yalkut Shimoni (2 Kings 237) records Rav and Shmuel disputing the wisdom of a different emperor's policies. In 2 Kings 18:31-2, the besieging Sancheriv tells the defenders of Yerushalayim not to be seduced by Chizkiyahu's promise of victory; instead, they should surrender, and he will exile them to "a land like your land; a land of grain and wine, a land of bread and vineyards, a land of olive oil and honey". Rav and Shmuel dispute whether Sancheriv was clever or foolish promising an equal rather than a better land. One says that he as clever, as the Jews would not have believed a bigger promise; the other says that he was foolish, because this way the Jews could simply shrug off the offer by saying they had nothing to gain.

All these disputes exist and are seen worthy of preserving **even though we know the outcome of the relevant policies.** Sancheriv does not succeed in getting Jews to open the gates for him, and then his army is destroyed by plague. So on what basis do we call him wise? Achashverosh successfully holds onto all 127 provinces without notable rebellions near or far. So on what basis do we call him foolish?

The best answer is that Rav and Shmuel were not learning policy from the texts – they were using their political experiences to prevent us from misreading the texts. Sancheriv was not successful, but we

shouldn't learn from that that overpromising is the only route to success, because reality shows us otherwise; Achashverosh was successful in preventing rebellion, but we **shouldn't learn from that** that taking one's base for granted is the only route to success, because reality shows us otherwise.

Once we know political cause-and-effect in the real world with absolute certainty, we can of course derive lessons with confidence from the text on that basis. For example, based on my analysis above, we can learn that the best way to Jewish unity in an environment rife with conspiracy theories is to call for a public fast whose purpose can be understood in very different ways.

Or maybe, just maybe, we should recognize that we can never know political cause-and-effect with certainty in the real world, and we should therefore be deeply suspicious of any claims that texts can dictate political strategy.

That doesn't mean that texts have no role in shaping our thinking. But I suggest that we err on the side of humility.